Women's Fiction Authors

Women's Fiction Authors: A Research Guide

Rebecca Vnuk

Author Research Series
Jen Stevens, Series Editor

LIBRARIES UNLIMITED
An Imprint of ABC-CLIO, LLC

A B C $\bullet$ C L I O

Santa Barbara, California • Denver, Colorado • Oxford, England

JAN 2010

Library of Congress Cataloging-in-Publication Data
Vnuk, Rebecca.
   Women's fiction authors : a research guide / Rebecca Vnuk.
       p. cm. — (Author research series)
   Includes bibliographical references and index.
     ISBN 978-1-59158-642-5 (hardcover : alk. paper)   1. Women—Fiction—Information
resources.   2. American fiction—Women authors—Bio-bibliography—Dictionaries.
3. English fiction—Women authors—Bio-bibliography—Dictionaries.   4. Chick
lit—Bio-bibliography—Dictionaries.   5. Women authors, American—20th
century—Biography—Dictionaries.   6. Women authors, American—21st century—
Biography—Dictionaries.   7. Women authors, English—20th century—Biography—
Dictionaries.   8. Women authors, English—21st century—Biography—Dictionaries.   I. Title.
   Z1231.W85V59   2009
   [PS374.W6]
   016.3054'2—dc22   2009015546

13   12   11   10   09   1   2   3   4   5

This book is also available on the World Wide Web as an eBook.
Visit www.abc-clio.com for details.

ABC-CLIO, LLC
130 Cremona Drive, P.O. Box 1911
Santa Barbara, California 93116-1911

This book is printed on acid-free paper ∞
Manufactured in the United States of America

Contents

Acknowledgments

I would like to thank the wonderful reader's advisory librarians I have had the pleasure to know—most especially the dedicated members of the Adult Reading Round Table in Illinois. Special thanks to Eugenia Bryant and Merle Jacob for their mentoring, friendship, and for giving me opportunities to practice the craft. Thank you to Libraries Unlimited editor Barbara Ittner and series editor Jen Stevens for their assistance and patience; and thank you to Mom, Dad, and Ken.

Introduction

Women's Fiction Authors: A Research Guide, part of the Author Research series, is intended for those who already know a given writer and want to learn more about that writer and/or find similar authors. However, you may also wish to simply browse through the guide to see who looks interesting. This guide is meant for librarians, students, and fans.

With this volume in the Author Research series, I've tried to give a nod to the many fine women's fiction authors who do not appear in classic reference works, and to gather the information that's available online in one easily accessible resource. Overall, I hope this book inspires readers try a new author, to find something they may not have read before, and to thoroughly enjoy getting lost in a good book.

Women's Fiction Defined

There is some debate over whether women's fiction is actually a genre in and of itself. Perhaps it is better to simply call it a *category* of books. The stories can follow any number of directions—they can be romantic, they can be suspenseful, they can be funny, they can be sad, but the thread holding them together is that the central character or characters are women. And the main thrust of the story is the life of that woman, rather than being all suspense, for example. These are novels exploring the lives of female protagonists, with a focus on their relationships with family, friends, and lovers.

Some books are characterized by a romantic tone—there may be elements of adventure or mystery as well, but the main theme is of a woman overcoming and learning from crises and emerging triumphant. One current trend is to employ a lighter, sometimes even tongue-in-cheek tone. But overall, emotions and relationships are the common thread between books that can be classified in this category.

Harper Collins/Avon senior editor Micki Nuding explains, "Women's Fiction can be commercial (and usually is) or literary; it can be here-and-now contemporary or a multigenerational saga. The woman is the star of the story and her changes and emotional development are the subject."[1]

So how do you know if a book is a romance or women's fiction? After all, the characters do fall in love in a large percentage of women's fiction novels. And boyfriends, husbands, and lovers show up as main characters as well.

For starters, a man (or a hero) might be waiting for the heroine of these novels at the end of her journey, but he does not usually get equal time or equal depth to his internal journey during the course of a book. In romance fiction, the author renders the hero in every detail in response to the expectations of readers. Another expectation in romance is the "happy ever after" ending, which does not matter in women's fiction.

Literary fiction is another category that can be argued over. Can women's fiction be serious, can it have lush language, or does that move it over to literary fiction? Again, this is one of the thorny issues with defining genres, as every reader has a different reaction to the appeal characteristics. There is plenty of literary fiction that has heart and soul to the story, but just because a novel is written by a woman and has female protagonists, it doesn't mean it has the same style and appeal that would make it women's fiction. Further muddying the waters, it's also quite possible for a book to fit into more than one category.

History and Trends

We've come a long way, baby, since the days when women wrote under a male pen name or used their initials in order to get their work published. Early feminist writers and 19th-century writers can be credited with the creation of the domestic fiction genre. Louisa May Alcott, Jane Austen, Willa Cather, and Rebecca West wrote about the women of their times and what they were going through as far as family and relationships were concerned. In the 1920s and 1930s, Edna Ferber's epic novels, such as *Show Boat* and *So Big* featured strong female protagonists and entertaining plots. Readers in the mid-19th century enjoyed stories of scandal and struggle, such as Mary McCarthy's *The Group* and Jacqueline Susann's *Valley of the Dolls.* By the 1970s, feminist fiction rose to the top of the bestseller lists, including *Wifey* by Judy Blume and *The Women's Room* by Marilyn French. The 1980s, the decade of big hair and big shoulder pads, brought big fiction as well, with women relishing the over-the-top characters and soap-opera storylines of the glitz and glamour novels of Jackie Collins and Judith Krantz, among others.

There are two subgroups of women's fiction that have gained popularity in the last decade. Chick lit, kicked off in the late 1990s with *Bridget Jones's*

Diary by Helen Fielding, is a sub-genre with titles focusing on single, 20- or 30-something protagonists usually trying to find their way in life, in the big city or in a new fabulous career. These books are humorous and generally lighthearted. (And if there are shoes or legs on the cover, you know that's what you're reading.)

There has been a lot of talk regarding the demise of chick lit, but the publishers keep them coming, and women keep reading them. There has been plenty of criticism of chick lit as well. After all, once chick lit became hot, authors scrambled to write their frothy, fun commercial successes at breakneck speed, publishers rushed to put them out, and before long, the market was saturated with books that looked and sounded alike, far too many for the consumer to process. And so, the trend ends, and in some cases, crashes hard. However, there has been quite a bit of branching out from the single-in-the-city books, with mommy lit dominating the publishing houses recently. And there has been a smooth blurring of the edges—it's often harder these days to pigeon hole something as chick lit instead of simply women's fiction.

On the flip side from chick lit, issue-driven titles are darker, dealing with family problems and issues—more hot topic, Oprah-esque tales. Issue-driven novels continue to increase in popularity, even without the assistance of Oprah's book club.

In recent years, ensemble fiction has begun to gain new ground. These are books that focus on a group of women brought together by a common bond—from craft circles, to book clubs, to college friends reuniting. Again, this speaks to the appeal of women wanting to read about characters who are like themselves, or who they would like to be.

While there are several awards for romantic fiction, such as the Romance Writers of America's RITA and Golden Heart awards, the only award currently given specifically for women's fiction is the Rona Jaffe Foundation Writer's Award. Meant for emerging authors, it has not been given to any of the authors featured in this book. However, it should be noted that several of the authors featured in this book have been awarded RITAs, various ALA awards, regional book awards, National Book Award citations, and more. These are mentioned in the individual author biographies.

Organization of Entries

Author entries are arranged in alphabetical order by the author's last name. Each author entry includes a short biographical sketch and information about the author's novels as well as biographical and critical information about them. You may notice that the vast majority of this information is from Web sites. Because of the relative newness of women's fiction as a recognized category, there are few print materials or scholarly works that focus only on women's fiction.

The following abbreviations are used for common general reference works that contain information on the authors profiled here:

> CA—*Contemporary Authors,* Gale (main source consulted for this book is the database version, *Contemporary Authors Online*)
> CLC—*Contemporary Literary Criticism*, Gale
> TCRHW—*Twentieth-Century Romance and Historical Writers*, 3rd edition, St. James, 1994.

For complete bibliographic information on these titles, please refer to the General Bibliography.

With some entries you'll find sections that suggest similar books and authors to try (i.e., "if you like Maeve Binchy, then you might like . . ."). Each entry also has been assigned categories that you can use to find authors who write similar types of books (i.e., sagas, family stories, etc.)

Selection Criteria

One of the most difficult aspects of writing this volume was deciding who to include and who to leave out. Purists will note that early authors are not represented here, and that was a conscious choice. Entire college courses, let alone shelves of reference books, are devoted to authors such as Jane Austen, Louisa May Alcott, and other important women writers. The choice for this book was then to focus on contemporary authors, those who do not normally get much coverage. Although a few classic women's fiction authors are covered here, we focused on writers for whom finding research materials might be more challenging.

The question of what makes women's fiction different from romance is also a difficult one to tackle. After all, romance writers are worthy of an entire book of their own. The effort was made to focus on writers who may have romantic elements in their stories, but who focus on the deeper relationships of women and the world around them, and not on sex or romantic love alone. Literary fiction is another tough call, and readers will note there are many authors not represented because they are more literary in tone. While there are one or two more literary authors represented here, some readers may wonder why the likes of Margaret Atwood, A. S. Byatt, or Anita Brookner are not represented. Again, the thought is that there are many individual reference works available on these authors, and they don't have quite the same feel as Danielle Steel or Barbara Delinsky, for example. I would argue the point that when readers are looking for women's fiction as a category, they are not looking to read the book for its language, description, or seriousness; instead they are looking for more of an escape, a good story, or relatable characters. Naturally, these criteria are subjective and can all be argued, however, to keep this from becoming a multivolume work, cuts had to be made.

Final considerations were the popularity, productivity, and appeal of an author. There are many fine authors not represented because they only have one or two novels currently published (Julia Glass and Ann Packer come to mind), they may not be as well-known as some of the others (chick lit authors Valerie Frankel and Wendy French are good examples), and finally, several writers were left out because they may fit better in other genre volumes (Jan Karon, Dee Henderson, Karen Kingsbury—inspirational; Mary Higgins Clark, Dorothy Gilman—mystery, Jennifer Crusie, Debbie Macomber, Fern Michaels—romance).

Some important authors not represented in this volume include:

Louisa May Alcott—classic
Margaret Atwood—literary
Jane Austen—classic
Charlotte Brontë—classic
Emily Brontë—classic
Anita Brookner—literary
A. S. Byatt—literary
Willa Cather—classic
Anita Diamant—literary
Louise Erdrich—literary
Kaye Gibbons—literary
Dee Henderson—inspirational, romance
Grace Livingston Hill—inspirational, romance
Eva Ibbotson—literary
Karen Kingsbury—inspirational
Barbara Kingsolver—literary
Debbie Macomber—romance
Mary McGarry Morris—literary
Fern Michaels—romance
Ann Patchett—literary
LaVyrle Spencer—romance

Note

1. Lisa Craig, "Women's Fiction vs. Romance: A Tale of Two Genres," *Writing-World.com,* http://www.writing-world.com/romance/craig.shtml. Last visited April 1, 2008.

Women's Fiction Timeline

Literary Events	World Events
1811–1815—Anonymously, Jane Austen publishes *Sense and Sensibility* (1811), *Pride and Prejudice* (1813), *Mansfield Park* (1814), and *Emma* (1815).	1811—Napoleon invades Russia. 1812—Great Britain and the United States engage in the War of 1812.
1871—George Eliot publishes her work under a male pseudonym to ensure her writing is taken seriously.	1865—The American Civil War comes to an end. 1871—The American Industrial Revolution begins.
1921—Edith Wharton becomes the first female author to win the Pulitzer Prize for Literature, for *The Age of Innocence.*	1920—The 19th Amendment is passed, and women earn the right to vote in the United States.
1936—One of the most popular books of all time, *Gone with the Wind* by Margaret Mitchell, is published, and is considered to be modern publishing's first blockbuster.	1930s—The United States is in the throes of the Great Depression. 1932—Amelia Earhart becomes the first woman to fly solo across the Atlantic Ocean.
1956—Grace Metalious's *Peyton Place* is published to much controversy (and is considered the second blockbuster novel of the 20th century.)	1950s—McCarthyism symbolizes a widespread social and cultural phenomenon of conservatism in America. 1950–1953—The Korean War.

Literary Events	World Events
1966—*Valley of the Dolls* by Jacqueline Susann is published.	1961—Use of the birth control pill becomes socially acceptable and widespread.
1977—Marilyn French's *The Women's Room* is published.	1973—Roe v. Wade passes.
1981—Jackie Collins's *Chances* ushers in an era of popular "glitz and glamour" novels for women.	1981—Ronald Reagan becomes President of the United States. 1986—The Chernobyl nuclear disaster occurs.
1989—Danielle Steel is listed in the Guinness Book of World Records for having a book on the New York Times Bestseller List for the most consecutive weeks of any author.	1989—The Berlin Wall comes down, a symbol of the end of Communism in Europe.
1996—Oprah Winfrey selects *The Deep End of the Ocean* by Jacquelyn Mitchard as the inaugural Oprah's Book Club pick.	1993—Bill Clinton becomes President of the United States.
1996—*Bridget Jones's Diary* by Helen Fielding is published, giving rise to the chick lit genre.	1997—Dolly the sheep is the first confirmed cloned mammal. Late 1990s—The rise of the Internet and the World Wide Web.
2002—*Good in Bed* is Jennifer Weiner's debut novel and signifies a more thoughtful shift in chick lit.	2001—Terrorists bomb the World Trade Center.
2008—Danielle Steel publishes her 75th novel, *Rogue*.	2008—Barack Obama is elected the first black President of the United States.

How to Use This Book

This book is intended for anyone who loves women's fiction—librarians, reader's advisors, book club leaders, and the general reader—anyone who wants to learn more about those who write it.

Fans (and Other Readers)

You can browse through to scope out potentially interesting authors and books to read. If you'd like to find out more about an author, check the "Biographies and Interviews" sections. An interview can be an especially fascinating way to get to know your favorite authors.

If you'd like to get a larger perspective on the vast body of women's fiction novels, check the "General Bibliography" appendix. Many general interest Web sites are listed that may lead you to more authors and new titles.

Students

You can browse through the book to get ideas to use for your projects and papers. Many of the authors listed here are hard to find in classic reference books, so this will hopefully be a good starting point for you. To find out more about an author's life, check out the "Biographies and Interviews" sections. "Web sites" sections will also lead to you interesting information about an author, including photos and blogs.

Librarians

The "Major Works" lists provide quick lists in chronological order by the authors to consult for reader's advisory questions. Some entries include a

"Read Alike" section that you can use to find books for the patron who has read all of their favorite author's books and needs more suggestions.

In turn, the "Biographies and Interviews," "Criticism and Readers' Guides," and "Web Sites" sections will provide useful for reference questions concerning writers and their works.

Book Club Leaders

You can browse through the book to find authors and books that your book club may be interested in. The "Biographies and Interviews" sections may be especially helpful to you for background information as you prepare for book club discussions. In addition, you will find a large number of reader's guides and discussion questions available in the "Criticism and Readers' Guides" sections.

What to Do If the Web Site Links Don't Work

Every effort has been made to make sure that the Web site links are current, but URLs do often change over time. If you should come across a URL that doesn't work, try the following:

- First, try a different Web browser. Some pages won't work in particular browsers.
- Next, try looking up the title of the page on an Internet search engine such as www.google.com. Google also caches sites, so try the cache links if the current link doesn't work.
- If it's a page from a publisher's Web site or a newspaper/magazine site, try doing an internal search in the Web site.
- Finally, try looking up the nonworking URL in the Internet Archive (www. archive.org), an online archive for both active and obsolete Web sites. The archive doesn't have every page that's ever been online, but has a large number of them.

Alphabetical List of Authors

Cecelia Ahern
Charlotte Vale Allen
Julia Alvarez
Mary Kay Andrews
Lois Battle
Elizabeth Berg
Maeve Binchy
Barbara Taylor Bradford
Connie Briscoe
Sandra Brown
Elizabeth Buchan
Meg Cabot
Elizabeth Cadell
Jennifer Chiaverini
Pearl Cleage
Jackie Collins
Claire Cook
Catherine Cookson
Barbara Delinsky
Katie Fforde
Helen Fielding
Joy Fielding
Fannie Flagg
Dorothea Benton Frank
Patricia Gaffney
Gail Godwin

Olivia Goldsmith
Eileen Goudge
Jane Green
Kristin Hannah
Joanne Harris
Jane Heller
Lynne Hinton
Alice Hoffman
Ann Hood
Rona Jaffe
Cathy Kelly
Marian Keyes
Cassandra King
Sophie Kinsella
Judith Krantz
Lorna Landvik
Billie Letts
Elinor Lipman
Jill McCorkle
Diane McKinney-Whetstone
Terry McMillan
Mameve Medwed
Sue Miller
Jacquelyn Mitchard
Sarah Mlynowski
Mary Alice Monroe

Jodi Picoult

Rosamunde Pilcher

Belva Plain

Anna Quindlen

Jeanne Ray

Luanne Rice

Nora Roberts

Ann B. Ross

Anita Shreve

Anne Rivers Siddons

Haywood Smith

Lee Smith

Danielle Steel

Amy Tan

Nancy Thayer

Adriana Trigiani

Joanna Trollope

Penny Vincenzi

Jennifer Weiner

Rebecca Wells

Marcia Willett

Meg Wolitzer

Laura Zigman

Women's Fiction Authors

Cecelia Ahern (1981–)
Chick Lit; Light
Biographical Sketch

Cecelia Ahern was born on September 30, 1981, in Dublin, Ireland. The daughter of the current Irish Prime Minister, she received a journalism degree, but went on to publish her first novel, *P.S. I Love You,* at age 21. Three more novels followed quickly; and *P.S. I Love You* was made into a movie in 2007.

Ahern's books feature Irish settings, strong young female characters, humor, and a sense of whimsy. While her first two novels were decidedly chick lit, her two most recent books have a fairy-tale, fantasy quality about them. She is also a co-creator and writer on the ABC television series, "Samantha Who?" Ahern lives in Dublin, Ireland.

My opinion of a fairy tale was of a story that lacked realism, in which female characters are "rescued" by men, whisked off their feet from the boredom of their mundane lives, proposed to, and brought to a castle where they would live happily ever after. This is not the case with my books. I want them to be about strong women. They are about real people with ordinary, everyday struggles who are faced with having to embark on a journey of self-discovery. (Cecelia Ahern, *Bookreporter* interview. http://www.bookreporter.com/authors/au-ahern-cecelia.aspLast visited June 26, 2008)

Major Works

Novels

P.S. I Love You (2004)
Rosie Dunne (2004)

If You Could See Me Now (2006)
There's No Place Like Here (2008)

Research Sources

Biographies and Interviews

Barker, Olivia. "Young Irish Lass Cecelia Ahern Off and Running in USA."
    USA Today. January 2, 2008. http://www.usatoday.com/life/books/news/
    2008–01–02-ahern_N.htm. Last visited March 13, 2008.
"Cecelia Ahern." *Bookreporter.* August 2006. http://www.bookreporter.com/
    authors/au-ahern-cecelia.asp. Last visited January 29, 2008. "Author Talk"
    interview with Ahern.
"Young People Who Rock: Cecelia Ahern." *CNN.com.* http://www.cnn.com/
    exchange/blogs/ypwr/2007/12/cecelia-ahern.html. Last visited January 29,
    2008. Video interview with Ahern.

Web Sites

"Cecelia Ahern." *Hyperion* http://www.ceceliaahernbooks.com/. U.S. Pub-
    lisher's Web site, featuring Q & A section, bibliography of U.S. titles, and
    reading group section.
Cecelia Ahern Official Web Site. http://www.ceceliaahern.ie/. Author's official
    Web site, featuring news updates, biography, and book information.

Charlotte Vale Allen (1941–)
Mainstream
Biographical Sketch

Born on January 19, 1941, in Toronto, Canada, Charlotte Vale Allen later
worked in England as an actress and singer. She came to the United States in
1966. Sexually abused as a child, she often includes different facets of abuse
and recovery in her novels; she also lectures extensively on the subject. Her
autobiography, *Daddy's Girl,* details an almost intolerable childhood as the
victim of abuse.

   One of the most successful Canadian-born novelists, her stories feature
dynamic women in difficult situations. She has also written under the pseudonym Katherine Marlowe. In 2006, she decided the publishing world had got-
ten too difficult, so she gave up on selling her last manuscripts and considers
herself "involuntarily retired." She owns the rights to her backlist and started
an independent publishing company, Island Nation, to reissue her titles for
the library market. Allen lives in Connecticut.

   My strongest ability as a writer is to make women real, to take you inside their heads and let you know how they feel, and to make you care

about them. (Charlotte Vale Allen, www.charlottevaleallen.com. Last visited June 26, 2008)

Major Works

Novels

Love Life (1976)
Hidden Meanings (1976)
Sweeter Music (1976)
Gentle Stranger (1977)
Mixed Emotions (1977)
Running Away (1977)
Meet Me in Time (1978)
Julia's Sister (1978)
Becoming (1978)
Believing in Giants (1978)
Gifts of Love (1978)
Acts of Kindness (1979)
Moments of Meaning (1979)
Times of Triumph (1979)
Promises (1980)
The Marmalade Man (1981)
Perfect Fools (1981)
Intimate Friends (1983)
Matters of the Heart (1985)
Time/Steps (1986)
Illusions (1987)
Dream Train (1988)
Night Magic (1989)
Painted Lives (1990)
Leftover Dreams (1992)
Dreaming in Color (1993)
Somebody's Baby (1995)
Claudia's Shadow (1996)
Mood Indigo (1997)
Parting Gifts (2001)
Grace Notes (2002)
Fresh Air (2003)
Sudden Moves (2004)

Other Works of Interest

Daddy's Girl. New York: Wyndam Books, 1980.
"Charlotte Vale Allen on Writing." *Charlotte Vale Allen.* http://www.char lottevaleallen.com/on_writing/. Last visited February 3, 2008.

Research Sources

Encyclopedias and Handbooks: CA

Biographies and Interviews

"Charlotte Vale Allen." *Contemporary Romance Writers.* http://contemporary
romancewriters.com/Authorinfo.cfm?authorID=4490 . Last visited February 3, 2008. Brief biography and booklist.
Crosbie, Lynn. "Don't Fence Me In." *Quill and Quire.* July 1996. http://www.
quillandquire.com/authors/profile.cfm?article_id=347 Last visited February 3, 2008.

Web Sites

Charlotte Vale Allen Official Web Site. http://www.charlottevaleallen.com/.
Last visited February 3, 2008. Features biography, full list of books, and several full text articles about the author.

Julia Alvarez (1950–)
Mainstream
Biographical Sketch

Julia Alvarez was born on March 27, 1950, in New York City, but grew up in the Dominican Republic. Her family was very involved in social and political matters, and Alvarez's father, who was involved in an underground movement to rid the Dominican Republic of its dictator, was a target for assassination. In 1960, the family returned to New York fleeing from the harsh dictatorship. A natural storyteller, Alvarez always wanted to be a writer and received degrees in creative writing from Middlebury College and Syracuse University. Her novels feature strong Hispanic women and have themes of identity and society. She is also a highly regarded poet, and has written several children's books.

Alvarez and her husband own a cooperative coffee farm in the Dominican Republic, where they started a school. She currently lives in Vermont.

[On the publication of her first novel, hailed as a "new voice"] I was forty-one with twenty-plus years of writing behind me. I often mention this to student writers who are discouraged at 19 when they don't have a book contract! (Julia Alvarez, http://www.juliaalvarez.com. Last visited June 26, 2008.)

Major Works

Novels

Homecoming (1984)
In the Time of the Butterflies (1994)

How the Garcia Girls Lost their Accents (1990)
Yo! (1997)
In the Name of Salome (2000)
Saving the World (2006)

Poetry Collections

Homecoming: New and Collected Poems (1996)
The Other Side: El Otro Lado (1996)
The Woman I Kept to Myself: Poems (2004)

Other Works of Interest

Something to Declare. Chapel Hill, NC: Algonquin Books. 1998.
"I Too, Sing America." *Writers on America.* http://usinfo.state.gov/products/
pubs/writers/alvarez.htm. Last visited February 3, 2008.

Research Sources

Encyclopedias and Handbooks: CA

"Julia Alvarez," *Dictionary of Literary Biography Vol. 282: New Formalist Poets.*
Detroit, MI: Gale, 2003. pp. 16–23.

Biographies and Interviews

Birnbaum, Robert. "Julia Alvarez." *Identity Theory.* May 22, 2006. http.//www.
identitytheory.com/interviews/birnbaum171.php. Last visited February 13,
2008.
Johnson, Ronie-Richele Garcia. "Julia Alvarez." *Las Mujeres.* http://www.las
mujeres.com/juliaalvarez/profile.shtml. Last visited February 13, 2008.
"Julia Alvarez." *Bookreporter.com.* September 22, 2000. http://www.book
reporter.com/authors/au-alvarez-julia.asp. Last visited February 4, 2008.
"Julia Alvarez." *Voices from the Gap.* August 6, 2004. http://voices.cla.umn.
edu/vg/Bios/entries/alvarez_julia.html. Last visited February 16, 2008.
Saldana, Matt. "Author Julia Alvarez on Censorship." *Independent Weekly.*
February 6, 2008. http://www.indyweek.com/gyrobase/Content?oid=oid%
3A173317. Last visited February 16, 2008.

Criticism and Readers' Guides

Bess, Jennifer. "Imploding the Miranda Complex in Julia Alvarez's How the
García Girls Lost Their Accents." *College Literature* (34:1) 2007, 78–105.
Reader's guide for *In the Time of the Butterflies. Penguin.* http://us.penguin
group.com/static/rguides/us/time_of_the_butterflies.html. Last visited February 20, 2008.

Reading group guide for *Saving the World*. *Reading Group Guides*. http:// www.readinggroupguides.com/guides3/saving_the_world1.asp. Last visited February 20, 2008.

Sirias, Silvio. *Julia Alvarez: A Critical Companion*. Westport, CT: Greenwood. 2001.

Walker, Susan. "Julia Alvarez." *Emory University English Department*. http://www. english.emory.edu/Bahri/Alvarez.html. Last visited February 14, 2008.

Web Sites

Finca Alta Gracia. http://www.cafealtagracia.com/. Last visited February 13, 2008. Web site of author's farm and business in the Dominican Republic.

Julia Alvarez Official Web Site. http://www.juliaalvarez.com/. Last visited February 14, 2008. Features extensive autobiographical essays, news, photographs, and information on her writings.

Mary Kay Andrews (1954–)
Humorous; Women's Romantic Fiction
Biographical Sketch

Mary Kay Andrews is the pseudonym that mystery writer Kathy Hogan Trocheck uses when writing women's fiction. She was born on July 27, 1954, in St. Petersburg, Florida. She worked as a journalist in Georgia for several years, notably covering the murder trials that inspired the nonfiction book and movie *Midnight in the Garden of Good and Evil*.

Under her real name, she writes two mystery series. Her women's fiction is all written under the name Mary Kay Andrews (a merging of her children's names). Her novels feature feisty heroines, plenty of snappy dialogue, humorous situations, Southern settings, and a spark of romance. She teaches writing classes and workshops, and lives in Atlanta, Georgia.

> To a writer, the happiest words in the English language are THE END. Although, royalty check is another fabulous phrase. (Mary Kay Andrews, http://www.marykayandrews.com/content/newsletter.asp. Last visited June 26, 2008.)

Major Works
Novels

Savannah Blues (2002)
Little Bitty Lies (2003)
Hissy Fit (2004)
Breeze Inn (2006)

Blue Christmas (2006)
Deep Dish (2008)

Research Sources

Biographies and Interviews

"Inside Mary Kay Andrews' Home in Avondale Estates." *AJC Homefinder.* http://projects.ajchomefinder.com/gallery/view/homes/private-quarters/pqtrocheck1209/. Last visited February 18, 2008. Photo tour of Andrew's historic home.

"Mary Kay Andrews." *Barnes and Noble Meet the Writers.* http://www.barnesandnoble.com/writers/writerdetails.asp?cid=1613524&z=y. Last visited February 18, 2008.

"Mary Kay Andrews." *Bookreporter.com.* March 21, 2008. http://www.bookreporter.com/authors/au-andrews-mary-kay.asp. Last visited May 16, 2008. Brief biography and several interviews.

"Mary Kay Andrews." *HarperCollins.* http://www.harpercollins.com/author/authorExtra.aspx?authorID=20217&isbn13=9780060519131&displayType=bookinterview. Last visited May 16, 2008.

"Mary Kay Andrews Interview." *Reading Group Guides.* 2002. http://www.readinggroupguides.com/roundtable/interview-andrews-mary-kay.asp. Last visited May 16, 2008.

Morris, Anne. "Behind Closed Doors." *BookPage.* March 2008. http://www.BookPage.com/0308bp/mary_kay_andrews.html. Last visited February 18, 2008.

Morris, Amy "Author Mary Kay Andrews: When They See the Cover, They Want it Like Candy." *Savannah Now.* February 11, 2007. http://savannahnow.com/node/225420. Last visited February 18, 2008.

Criticism and Readers' Guides

Reading group guide for *Hissy Fit. Reading Group Guides.* http://www.readinggroupguides.com/guides3/hissy_fit1.asp. Last visited February 18, 2008.

Reading guide for *Savannah Breeze. HarperCollins.* http://www.harpercollins.com/author/authorExtra.aspx?isbn13=9780060564667&displayType=readingGuide. Last visited February 18, 2008.

Reading guide for *Blue Christmas.* HarperCollins. http://www.harpercollins.com/author/authorExtra.aspx?isbn13=9780061370489&displayType=readingGuide. Last visited November 18, 2008.

Web Sites

Kathy Hogan Trocheck Official Web Site. http://www.kathytrocheck.com. Last visited February 18, 2008.

Mary Kay Andrews Official Web Site http://www.marykayandrews.com/. Features biography, newsletter, book information. Last visited February 18, 2008.
Myspace. "Mary Kay Andrews." http://profile.myspace.com/index.cfm?fuse action=user.viewprofile&friendID=74903736. Last visited February 18, 2008. Andrew's official MySpace page.

Lois Battle (1942–)
Historical; Mainstream
Biographical Sketch

Lois Battle was born on October 6, 1942, in Subiaco, Australia. Her family moved to the United States in 1945; and in 1958 she moved to New York City to study drama. After acting in commercials, television, films, and off-Broadway plays, she changed to a writing career in the 1980s. Battle's novels feature strong women, relationships, and Southern settings. They range from historical sagas to contemporary settings.

Battle does not grant many interviews and does not have a personal Web site. Her last novel was written in 2001, and her publisher has no current plans for the next book. She currently lives in Beaufort, South Carolina.

> I felt the issue of not having a man could be more dramatically drawn for women in the South. (Lois Battle, *Publishers Weekly,* interview 1993)

Major Works

Novels

Season of Change (1980)
War Brides (1982)
Southern Women (1984)
A Habit of the Blood (1987)
The Past Is Another Country (1990)
Storyville (1993)
Bed & Breakfast (1996)
The Florabama Ladies' Auxiliary & Sewing Circle (2001)

Research Sources

Encyclopedias and Handbooks: CA; TCRHW

Biographies and Interviews

Robertson, Brewster. "Lois Battle: Having Given Up an Acting Career, She Creates Heroines Who Make Difficult Choices." *Publishers Weekly* (240:2), (January 11, 1993), 43–44.

Criticism and Readers' Guides

Reading group guide for *The Florabama Ladies' Auxiliary & Sewing Circle.* *Reading Group Guides.* http://www.readinggroupguides.com/guides3/flo rabama_ladies_auxiliary1.asp. Last visited January 20, 2008.

Web Sites

"Lois Battle." *Internet Movie Database.* http://www.imdb.com/name/nm0061517/. Last visited January 20, 2008. Acting credentials for Lois Battle.

Elizabeth Berg
Mainstream
Biographical Sketch

Elizabeth Berg was born on December 2, 1948, in St. Paul, Minnesota. Because her father was in the U.S. Army, her family moved to a new city every couple of years. She became a registered nurse, and then subsequently left her career to care for her two young daughters. That's when she began to write. She published her first novel, *Durable Goods,* in 1993, in which she plays heavily on her own experience as an "army brat."

Berg's novels focus on relationships, from friends to families to lovers. She writes about everyday life, tragedies large and small, and the search for happiness in its many forms. She has won several awards for her writing, including New England Book Award for fiction in 1997 for her body of work; two Best Book of the Year awards from the American Library Association for *Durable Goods* and *Joy School. Open House* was an Oprah's Book Club selection; and in 2000, her novel *Range of Motion* was made into a television movie for the Lifetime network. She lives in Oak Park, Illinois.

> First and foremost, a lesson I learned from being a nurse is how important seemingly ordinary life is, which of course is not ordinary at all, and how much is held in the smallest of things. (Elizabeth Berg, *Other Voices* interview. http://webdelsol.com/Other_Voices/BergInt.htm. Last visited June 26, 2008)

Major Works

Novels

Durable Goods (1993)
Talk before Sleep (1994)
Range of Motion (1995)
The Pull of the Moon (1996)

Joy School (1997)
What We Keep (1998)
Until the Real Thing Comes Along (1999)
Open House (2000)
Never Change (2001)
Say When (2003)
The Art of Mending (2004)
The Year of Pleasures (2005)
We Are All Welcome Here (2006)
The Handmaid and the Carpenter (2006)
Dream When You're Feeling Blue (2007)

Short-Story Collection

The Day I Ate Whatever I Wanted and Other Small Acts of Liberation (2008)

Research Sources

Encyclopedias and Handbooks: CA

"Elizabeth Berg," in *Dictionary of Literary Biography, Volume 292: Twenty-First-Century American Novelists*. Detroit, MI: Gale, 2004. pp. 10–15.

Biographies and Interviews

"A Conversation with Elizabeth Berg about *Open House.*" *BookBrowse.* http://www.bookbrowse.com/author_interviews/full/index.cfm?author_number=471. Last visited June 26, 2008.

"Elizabeth Berg." *Barnes and Noble Meet the Writers.* http://www.barnesandnoble.com/writers/writerdetails.asp?cid=883100. Last visited June 26, 2008.

McDonald, Craig. "True to Form." *Art of the Word.* June 2002. http://www.modestyarbor.com/elizabethberg.html. Last visited June 26, 2008.

"Meet the Author: Elizabeth Berg" *Public Library of Charlotte and Mecklenburg County Readers Club.* 2004. http://www.readersclub.org/meetAuthor.asp?author=11. Last visited June 23, 2008. Features Q&A and podcast.

Shoup, Barbara. "Barbara Shoup talks with Elizabeth Berg." *Other Voices #40. Web Del Sol.* http://webdelsol.com/Other_Voices/BergInt.htm. Last visited June 26, 2008.

Criticism and Readers' Guides

Reading group guide for *The Art of Mending. Reading Group Guides.* http://www.readinggroupguides.com/guides3/art_of_mending2.asp. Last visited June 26, 2008.

Reading group guide for *Open House Reading Group Guides*. http://www.
readinggroupguides.com/guides_O/open_house1.asp. Last visited June 26,
2008.

Reading group guide for *Talk Before Sleep. Reading Group Guides*. http://
www.randomhouse.com/catalog/display.pperl?isbn=9780345491251&
view=rg. Last visited June 26, 2008.

Web Sites

"Elizabeth Berg." *Random House*. http://www.randomhouse.com/author/
results.pperl?authorid=2048. Official publisher Web site featuring book
information and brief biography.

Elizabeth Berg Official Web Site. http://www.elizabeth-berg.net/. Last visited
June 26, 2008. Features book information, blog, podcast of an author
reading, photographs, and calendar of appearances.

If You Like Elizabeth Berg

Elizabeth Berg writes contemporary stories about average, everyday women
and families dealing with life in general. She has a good ear for dialogue and
makes her situations realistic and familiar. Her novels deal with a variety of
issues; for example, *Talk Before Sleep* tells the story of a friendship tested by
illness, whereas *Open House* showcases a woman dealing with divorce.

Then You Might Like

Ann Hood. Hood's novels feature similar themes—much like Berg, she writes
about women handling family issues, enjoying friendships, and dealing with
the complexities of life. Her debut novel *Somewhere Off the Coast of Maine*
features three friends struggling to reconnect with one another.

Elinor Lipman. Lipman is known for a sense of humor that's a little sharper
than Berg's; however, her novels feature realistic, everyday women dealing with
family and social issues. Her novels nicely capture their times, often acting as
social satire.

Jeanne Ray. Ray's novels also display more humor than Berg, but her stories
feature families and mature women dealing with the everyday ups and downs
of life. *Step-Ball-Change* and *Eat Cake* are good choices for Berg fans.

Luanne Rice. Rice's novels feature strong, intelligent women dealing with life's
everyday tragedies, much like Berg's. Family and friends are the showcased relationships in Rice's novels, such as *Stone Heart,* the story of a woman's return
to her home town where she discovers her sister's abusive family situation.

Anita Shreve. Shreve, although more literary than women's fiction authors,
showcases strong women that may appeal to women's fiction readers. They

may find her much darker, but may enjoy her stories of everyday women dealing with extraordinary circumstances. A good choice to start with would be *The Pilot's Wife,* the story of a woman confronted after her husband's death with his infidelity.

Joanna Trollope. Trollope's very British novels are set in an entirely different country than Berg's but her novels all focus on average, middle-class women dealing with anything from raising families to remarriage and other domestic dramas. Her novel *Marrying the Mistress* showcases a family dealing with the aftermath when their father marries his much younger mistress, who turns out to be a delightful woman.

Maeve Binchy
Family Stories; Gentle
Biographical Sketch

Maeve Binchy was born in on May 28, 1940, in Dalkey, Ireland. She often speaks about having a happy childhood living just outside of Dublin. In the 1960s, she taught history and foreign languages at a Dublin girl's school; and while on a trip to Israel in 1963, wrote letters home that her parents forwarded to the *Irish Times* and subsequently became a popular columnist for the paper before writing fiction.

Binchy's novels focus on family relationships, often featuring a large cast of characters, and are frequently set in Ireland. Her characters often seek independence or understanding. *Tara Road* was an Oprah's Book Club selection, and *Circle of Friends* was made into a movie in 1990. Binchy lives in Dalkey, Ireland, not far from the house she grew up in.

> I never wanted to write. I just wrote letters home from a kibbutz in Israel to reassure my parents that I was still alive and well fed and having a great time. They thought these letters were brilliant and sent them to a newspaper. So I became a writer by accident. (Maeve Binchy, *Guardian (UK)* interview. http://books.guardian.co.uk/whyiwrite/story/0,,2110875,00.html. Last visited June 26, 2008)

Major Works

Novels

Light a Penny Candle (1983)
Echoes (1985)
Firefly Summer (1988)
Silver Wedding (1989)

Circle of Friends (1990)
The Lilac Bus (1991)
The Copper Beech (1992)
The Glass Lake (1995)
Evening Class (1996)
Tara Road (1998)
Scarlet Feather (2001)
Quentins (2002)
Nights of Rain and Stars (2004)
Whitethorn Woods (2007)

Short-Story Collections

London Transports (1986)
This Year It Will Be Different and Other Stories: A Christmas Treasury (1996)
The Return Journey and Other Stories (1999)

Other Works of Interest

"Living Large." *Good Housekeeping.* May 2007. Available online at http://www.goodhousekeeping.com/names/blessings/maeve-binchy-overweight-may07. Last visited June 26, 2008. Essay by Binchy on the issue of weight.

Research Sources

Encyclopedias and Handbooks: CA; CLC

"Maeve Binchy" in *Dictionary of Literary Biography, Volume 319: British and Irish Short-Fiction Writers, 1945–2000.* Detroit, MI: Gale, 2005. pp. 34–38.

Biographies and Interviews

Kanner, Ellen. "Maeve Binchy: Finding the Heroes Among Ordinary People." *BookPage.* March 2001. http://www.bookpage.com/0103bp/maeve_binchy.html. Last visited June 26, 2008.

Kinson, Sarah. "Why I Write: Maeve Binchy." June 25, 2007. *The Guardian (UK).* http://books.guardian.co.uk/whyiwrite/story/0,,2110875,00.html. Last visited June 26, 2008.

"Maeve Binchy." *Bookreporter.* http://www.bookreporter.com/authors/au-binchy-maeve.asp. Last visited June 26, 2008.

Rabinovich, Dina. "The Story Seller" *The Guardian (UK).* September 1, 1998. Available online at http://books.guardian.co.uk/reviews/generalfiction/0,,96057,00.html. Last visited June 26, 2008.

Read Ireland. http://www.readireland.ie/aotm/Binchy.html. Brief biography and reviews of her books from an Irish bookseller.

Criticism and Readers' Guides

"Maeve Binchy" in *Contemporary Popular Writers.* Detroit, MI: St. James Press, 1997. p. 34–35.
"Maeve Binchy" in *Contemporary Novelists.* 7th ed. Detroit, MI: St. James Press, 2001. p. 107–108.
"Maeve Binchy," in *Major 21st-Century Writers. Vol. 1.* Detroit, MI: Gale, 2005.
Reading guide for *Whitethorn Woods. Random House.* http://www.random house.com/catalog/display.pperl?isbn=9780307265784&view=rg. Last visited June 26, 2008.

Web Sites

Maeve Binchy Official Web Site. http://www.maevebinchy.com/. Last visited June 26, 2008. Features book information and a short story.

If You Like Maeve Binchy

Maeve Binchy writes gentle, light stories set in Ireland, often featuring a large cast of characters. Her characters are recognizable and true-to-life. Her settings have a delightful small-town feel, even when she's writing about Dublin. She focuses on the interactions between her (sometimes eccentric) characters.

Then You Might Like

Elizabeth Cadell. Cadell is known for writing gentle romantic family stories. The plots of her novels often involve eccentric characters and an independent heroine. While they are more romantic in tone than Binchy's, her characters and realistic situations will appeal to Binchy fans.

Fannie Flagg. Flagg's stories may not be set in Ireland, but her small Southern towns featuring eccentric oddball characters are a good match for Binchy readers. Gentle and humorous, they evoke the same sense of community that Binchy is known for. A good title to start with would be *Welcome to the World, Baby Girl!,* the story of a young woman returning to her home town to uncover family secrets.

Lynne Hinton. Hinton writes novels that are thought of more as Christian fiction; they feature strong women and issues that relate to family and friendship. Her Hope Springs trilogy (*Friendship Cake, Hope Springs, Forever Friend*) features the very different ladies of a small North Carolina church, who begin the project of writing a cookbook and become unlikely friends. Also, like Binchy, Hinton uses intertwining characters and subplots in this series.

Cathy Kelly. While Kelly's novels are more contemporary and less gentle than Binchy, they wonderfully capture the feel of modern Ireland. Her stories focus more tightly on a smaller group of characters, as opposed to Binchy's style of incorporating many characters. Still, fans of Binchy will likely appreciate Kelly's touch with relationships and the everyday trials and tribulations of modern Irish women.

Rosamunde Pilcher. Although Pilcher's stories tend to be more romantic than Binchy's, they also feature large casts of characters who are often extended families. The English and Scottish settings will also appeal to Binchy fans.

Marcia Willett. Willett's novels, set in the rural West Country English countryside, feature mature women and their families. Willett's sense of leisurely pacing matches Binchy's gentle style. *A Week in Winter,* the charming story of an extended family dealing with the sale of the family farmhouse, would be a good choice for Binchy fans.

Barbara Taylor Bradford (1933–)
Historical; Saga; Women's Romantic Fiction
Biographical Sketch

Barbara Taylor Bradford was born on May 5, 1933, in Leeds, Yorkshire, England. She worked at the *Yorkshire Evening Post,* starting as a typist and working her way up to become the women's page editor at age 18, the youngest in all of England. She also worked as a columnist for the *London Evening News.* Bradford is very involved with a number of charities, including the March of Dimes and many others in the United Kingdom and United States. In June 2007, Bradford was awarded an OBE (The Order of the British Empire) for her contributions to literature.

Prior to writing fiction, Bradford published a number of nonfiction books on housekeeping and etiquette. Her novels feature strong women who overcome obstacles. Many of them are sweeping sagas that follow families through several generations. Ten of Bradford's novels have been made into television miniseries or movies. Her debut novel, *A Woman of Substance,* broke the record when it stayed on the paperback bestseller lists for over a year. She currently lives in Manhattan.

> My mother inspired all my desires to read and write. I was an only child and often alone. She encouraged me when I scribbled things. When I was 10, she sent a story I had written to the Children's Magazine and I got 10 shillings and sixpence for it. I told her then, that I wanted to be a writer. (Barbara Taylor Bradford, *Guardian (UK)* interview. http://www.guard ian.co.uk/books/2007/oct/22/whyiwrite. Last visited June 26, 2008.)

Major Works

Novels

Voice of the Heart (1983)
Act of Will (1986)
The Women in His Life (1990)
Remember (1991)
Angel (1993)
Everything to Gain (1994)
Dangerous to Know (1995)
Love in Another Town (1995)
Her Own Rules (1996)
A Secret Affair (1996)
Power of a Woman (1997)
A Sudden Change of Heart (1999)
Where You Belong (2000)
The Triumph of Katie Byrne (2001)
Three Weeks in Paris (2002)
Harte Family Saga: *A Woman of Substance* (1979), *Hold the Dream* (1985), *To Be the Best* (1988), *Emma's Secret* (2004), *Unexpected Blessings* (2005), *Just Rewards* (2006)
Ravenscar Trilogy: *The Ravenscar Dynasty* (2006), *The Heir* (2007), *Being Elizabeth* (2008)

Research Sources

Encyclopedias and Handbooks: CA; TCRHW

Biographies and Interviews

Cooke, Rachel. "You Can Never Be Too Rich." October 8, 2006. *The Observer.* http://www.guardian.co.uk/lifeandstyle/2006/oct/08/features.woman2. Last visited March 5, 2009.

Kinson, Sarah. "Why I Write: Barbara Taylor Bradford." October 22, 2007. *The Guardian.* http://www.guardian.co.uk/books/2007/oct/22/whyiwrite. Last visited March 5, 2009.

MacDonald, Jay. "Woman of Substance has Mysterious Past." May 23, 2007. *Bankrate.com.* http://www.bankrate.com/yho/news/investing/2007 0527_fame_fortune_barbara_bradford_a1.asp. Last visited March 5, 2009.

Criticism and Readers' Guides

"Barbara Taylor Bradford" in *Contemporary Popular Writers.* Detroit, MI: St. James Press, 1997. p. 43–44.

Dudgeon, Piers. *A Woman of Substance: The Life and Works of Barbara Taylor Bradford*. London, England: HarperCollins, 2005.
Reading group guide for *A Sudden Change of Heart. Reading Group Guides.* http://www.readinggroupguides.com/guides_S/sudden_change_of_heart1.asp. Last visited June 26, 2008.

Web Sites

Barbara Taylor Bradford Audio Webcast. *Library of Congress.* http://www.loc.gov/today/cyberlc/feature_wdesc.php?rec=3460. Last visited June 26, 2008. Video clip of Bradford at the 2002 National Book Festival.
Barbara Taylor Bradford Official Web Site. http://www.barbarataylorbradford.com/. Last visited June 26, 2008. Features biography, bibliographies, fan message board, and photo album.
FunTrivia.com. "Barbara Taylor Bradford Trivia." http://www.funtrivia.com/en/Literature/Bradford-Barbara-Taylor-8872.html. Last visited June 26, 2008. Features 20 trivia questions about her books.

If You Like Barbara Taylor Bradford

Barbara Taylor Bradford's early, heartwarming multigenerational sagas feature strong women who overcome obstacles to make it to the top.

Then You Might Like

Elizabeth Cadell. Cadell is more of a gentle read than Bradford, but was famous for her sweeping sagas, often set in exotic locales.

Catherine Cookson. Cookson's sagas feature northern English settings and strong female characters, usually struggling with British class differences. Her spirited and likable heroines will likely appeal to Bradford's readers as well.

Belva Plain. Plain is known for her sweeping, leisurely paced sagas featuring independent woman dealing with life.

Danielle Steel. Several of Steel's sagas would appeal to readers looking for a long, intimate look at a woman's life, such as *Zoya* or *Granny Dan.* Readers looking for the story of a woman's rise to fame would enjoy Steel's novel *Star.*

Penny Vincenzi. Vincenzi's novels are much more glitzy than Bradford's, however, her Spoils of Time Trilogy (*No Angel, Something Dangerous,* and *Into Temptation*) is a saga that follows a high-powered family through the years.

Connie Briscoe (1952–)
African American; Mainstream
Biographical Sketch

Connie Briscoe was born on December 31, 1952, in Washington, D.C. Briscoe was born with a genetic condition that caused hearing loss, and was profoundly deaf by her thirties. A cochlear implant restored much of her hearing. She worked in the magazine industry before writing full time, and was the managing editor for the *American Annals of the Deaf.*

Her books center on the personal struggles of contemporary middle-class African American women, covering romantic relationships, work issues, and family. She has also garnered acclaim for her nonfiction work featuring essays and photographs of famous black women in the arts, *Jewels: 50 Phenomenal Black Women Over 50*, published in 2007. Briscoe lives in Falls Church, Virginia.

> I'm not sure when I first thought about being a writer. I've always had "a way with words" and took a few stabs at writing a novel when I was in my twenties, but I never finished—perhaps because I did not have enough life experience to bring it to a satisfactory conclusion. (Connie Briscoe, http://www.hachettebookgroupusa.com/authors/36/3699/index. html. Last visited June 26, 2008)

Major Works

Novels

Sisters and Lovers (1994)
Big Girls Don't Cry (1996)
A Long Way from Home (1999)
P. G. County (2002)
Can't Get Enough (2005)

Research Sources

Encyclopedias and Handbooks: CA

Biographies and Interviews

Barnes, Stephanie. "Diamonds in the Rough." *Shades.* January 2008. http://shadeszine.com/index.php/2008/01/diamonds-in-the-rough/. Last visited June 26, 2008.

"Connie Briscoe on *Can't Get Enough.*" *Bill Thompson's Eye on Books.* http://www.eyeonbooks.com/ibp.php?ISBN=0385501625. Last visited June 26, 2008. Audio interview clip.

"Connie Briscoe on *P. G. County.*" *Bill Thompson's Eye on Books.* http://www. eyeonbooks.com/ibp.php?ISBN=0385501625. Last visited June 26, 2008. Audio interview clip.

"I Never Thought My Book Would Take Off!" *World Around You.* March– April 1997. http://clerccenter.gallaudet.edu/worldaroundyou/mar-apr97/ connie.html. Last visited June 26, 2008.

Criticism and Readers' Guides

Reader's guide for *Can't Get Enough. Random House.* http://www.random house.com/broadway/blackink/catalog/display.pperl?isbn=97807679212 99&view=rg. Last visited June 26, 2008.

Reading group guide for *Long Way from Home. Reading Group Guides.* http:// www.readinggroupguides.com/guides_L/long_way_from_home2.asp. Last visited June 26, 2008.

Web Sites

"Connie Briscoe." *Hatchette Book Group USA.* http://www.hachettebook groupusa.com/authors/36/3699/index.html. Last visited June 26, 2008. Official publisher Web site.

Connie Briscoe Official Web Site. http://conniebriscoe.com/. Last visited June 26, 2008. Features brief bio, bibliographies, blog, and "Connie Briscoe presents," featuring other writers and book industry professionals.

Sandra Brown (1948–)
Romantic Suspense; Women's Romantic Fiction
Biographical Sketch

Sandra Brown was born on March 12, 1948, in Waco, Texas. She worked in television and journalism before turning to a writing career. She began writing romances, and has published 70 novels, under her name as well as under the pseudonyms Rachel Ryan, Laura Jordan, and Erin St. Claire. Currently, she is best known for her novels, which successfully combine romance elements with mystery, thriller, and romantic suspense, and feature strong women characters.

Brown is the recipient of an American Business Women's Association's Distinguished Circle of Success award; the B'nai B'rith's Distinguished Literary Achievement Award; an A. C. Greene Award; the Texas Medal of Arts Award for Literature; and the Romance Writers of America's Lifetime Achievement Award. She lives in Arlington, Texas.

> Often I think about the characters in past books and wonder what they're up to these days, but never to the point of wanting to write another story about them. I admire writers who can keep a recurring character fresh

and interesting. I prefer resolving the problems of one set of characters, then moving on to the next. Otherwise, I think I'd get bored. (Sandra Brown, *Bookreporter* interview. 2004. http://www.bookreporter.com/au thors/au-brown-sandra.asp. Last visited June 30, 2008)

Major Works

Novels

The *Texas!* Trilogy: *Texas! Lucky* (1990), *Texas! Chase* (1991), *Texas! Sage* (1991).
The Alibi (1999)
Standoff (2000)
The Switch (2000)
Envy (2001)
The Crush (2002)
Hello, Darkness (2003)
White Hot (2004)
Chill Factor (2005)
Ricochet (2006)
Play Dirty (2007)
Smoke Screen (2008)

> A full, annotated printable list of Brown's books can be found on her Web site, at http://www.sandrabrown.net/books_search.php. A bibliography separated by series and linking to books under her pseudonyms can be found through Fantastic Fiction at http://www.fantasticfiction.co.uk/b/sandra-brown/.

Research Sources

Encyclopedias and Handbooks: CA; TCRHW

Biographies and Interviews

Ellis, Rick. "Q&A: Sandra Brown." *All Your TV.* http://allyourtv.com/0708 season/q&asandrabrown.html. Last visited June 30, 2008.
Holmes, Gina. "Interview with NYT Best-Selling Novelist, Sandra Brown." August 28, 2007. *Novel Journey.* http://noveljourney.blogspot.com/2007/08/interview-with-nyt-best-selling.html. Last visited June 30, 2008.
Mitchell, Sandy. "An Interview with Sandra Brown." August 14, 2007. *Suite 101.* http://mysterycrimefiction.suite101.com/article.cfm/an_interview_with_sandra_brown. Last visited June 30, 2008.
"Sandra Brown." *Barnes and Noble Meet the Writers.* http://www.barnesand noble.com/writers/writer.asp?cid=968797. Last visited June 30, 2008. Features brief bio, interview, and audio interview.

"Sandra Brown." *Bill Thompson's Eye on Books.* http://www.eyeonbooks. com/icp.php?authID=1287. Last visited June 26, 2008. Audio interview clip.

"Sandra Brown." *Bookreporter.com.* http://www.bookreporter.com/authors/ au-brown-sandra.asp. Last visited June 30, 2008. Brief bio and several interviews.

Web Sites

Sandra Brown Official Web Site. http://www.sandrabrown.net/index.htm. Last visited June 30, 2008. Features book list, biography, videos and photo gallery.

Elizabeth Buchan (1948–)
Women's Romantic Fiction

Biographical Sketch

Elizabeth Buchan was born on May 21, 1948, in Guildford, Surrey, England. To keep herself occupied while attending boarding school, she became a voracious reader and subsequently decided that she wanted to be a writer. Before publishing her own books, she worked as a fiction editor for Penguin Books and Random House. She has also written for magazines. In 1994, her novel *Consider the Lily,* a historical novel set in the 1930s, won the Romantic Novelist's Association Novel of the Year.

Her novels feature strong women and realistic storylines about the ups and downs of relationships. They cover a variety of time periods, from *Consider the Lily,* a historical novel set in the 1930s, to the more modern settings of *Revenge of the Middle-Aged Woman* and *The Good Wife.* Buchan currently lives in London.

> I always bear in mind that is [sic] if something has a life in it, then it is bound to be liked and disliked for the dual response is a reflection of human nature. It follows, then, that you have to believe absolutely in what you are writing and be prepared to stick by your vision. (Elizabeth Buchan, *WriteWords Writer's Community* interview. http://www.writewords. org.uk/interviews/elizabeth_buchan.asp. Last visited June 26, 2008)

Major Works

Novels

Daughters of the Storm (1990)
Light of the Moon (1991)
Consider the Lily (1993)
Perfect Love (1999)

Against Her Nature (1997)
Secrets of the Heart (2000)
Revenge of the Middle-Aged Woman (2003)
The Good Wife Strikes Back (2004)
Everything She Thought She Wanted (2005)
Wives Behaving Badly (2006)

Research Sources

Encyclopedias and Handbooks: CA

Biographies and Interviews

"Elizabeth Buchan." *Barnes and Noble Meet the Writers.* http://www.barnesand noble.com/writers/writer.asp?cid=1068334. Last visited June 26, 2008.

"Elizabeth Buchan." *Bookbrowse.* http://www.bookbrowse.com/author_ interviews/full/index.cfm?author_number=862. Last visited June 26, 2008.

"Elizabeth Buchan." *WriteWords Writer's Community.* August 31, 2007. http:// www.writewords.org.uk/interviews/elizabeth_buchan.asp . Last visited June 26, 2008.

Jesus, Diego X, and Mark London. "Introducing . . . Elizabeth Buchan and Beverly Walton-Porter." *Inkwell Newswatch.* January 2008. 0068ttp://www. fwointl.com/artman/exec/view.cgi?archive=20&num=436. Last visited June 26, 2008.

Memnott, Carol. "Middle-Aged Elizabeth Buchan Strikes Again." January 7, 2004. *USA Today.* Available online at http://www.usatoday.com/life/ books/reviews/2004–01–06-good-wife_x.htm. Last visited June 26, 2008.

Criticism and Readers' Guides

Discussion questions for *Consider the Lily. Readers Club of America.* http:// www.readersclubofamerica.com/consider_lily.htm. Last visited June 26, 2008.

Reader's guide for *The Good Wife Strikes Back. Penguin.* http://us.penguin group.com/static/rguides/us/good_wife_strikes_back.html. Last visited June 26, 2008.

Reading group guide for *Revenge of the Middle Aged Woman. Reading Group Guides.* http://www.readinggroupguides.com/guides3/revenge_of_the_ middle-aged_woman1.asp. Last visited June 26, 2008.

Web Sites

Elizabeth Buchan Official Web Site. http://www.elizabethbuchan.com/. Last visited June 26, 2008. Separate pages for U.K. readers and U.S. readers. Features bibliography, brief biography, diary, and reading guide links.

Meg Cabot (1967–)
Chick Lit; Humorous; Women's Romantic Fiction

Biographical Sketch

Meg Cabot was born on February 1, 1967, in Bloomington, Indiana. After attending New York University, she worked for 10 years as a residence hall manager before becoming a best-selling author. Her work spans many genres—preteen series, teen novels, adult romances (under the name Patricia Cabot), chick lit, and light mysteries. Her teen series *The Princess Diaries* has been made into a series of movies.

Cabot's chick lit features snappy dialogue, self-deprecating characters, humorous situations, and romance. The author lives in Indiana and New York City.

There are two types of writers: egg layers and egg polishers. I am such an egg layer. I turn in the first draft and I'm done. They come back to me with revisions, and I hate them. I know this sounds terrible, but the idea of working on a book for more than a month? That's torture. (Meg Cabot, *Publishers Weekly* interview. 2006. http://www.publishersweekly. com/article/CA6352841.html. Last visited June 27, 2008)

Major Works

Novels

The Boy Next Door (2002)
Boy Meets Girl (2004)
Every Boy's Got One (2005)
Heather Wells series: *Size 12 Is Not Fat: A Heather Wells Mystery* (2006), *Size 14 Is Not Fat Either* (2007), *Big Boned* (2008)
Queen of Babble series: *Queen of Babble* (2006), *Queen of Babble in the Big City* (2007), *Queen of Babble Gets Hitched* (2008)

Research Sources

Encyclopedias and Handbooks: CA

Biographies and Interviews

Coleman, Sandy. "Writer's Corner: Meg Cabot." July 5, 2007. *All About Romance.* http://www.likesbooks.com/cabot2007.html. Last visited June 27, 2008.
Corbett, Sue. "Meg Cabot in Margaritaville." *Publishers Weekly.* July 17, 2006. Available online at http://www.publishersweekly.com/article/CA6352841. html. Last visited June 27, 2008.

Sapet, Kerrily. "Meg Cabot." *Bookloons.* June 2006. http://www.bookloons. com/cgi-bin/Columns.asp?name=Meg%20Cabot&type=Interview. Last visited June 27, 2008.

Web Sites

"Meg Cabot." *Harper Collins.* http://www.harpercollins.com/authors/19546/ Meg_Cabot/index.aspx. Last visited June 27, 2008. Features video blog, author essays, and book information.
Meg Cabot Official Web Site. http://www.megcabot.com. Last visited June 27, 2008. Features complete bibliography, biography, fan message board, and blog.
"Meg Cabot Webcast." *Library of Congress.* http://www.loc.gov/bookfest/2005/ cabot.html. Last visited June 27, 2008. Video clip of Cabot at the 2005 National Book Fest.

If You Like Meg Cabot

Cabot's chick lit features snappy dialogue, self-deprecating characters, humorous situations, and romance.

Then You Might Like

Mary Kay Andrews. While they do not really qualify as chick lit, Andrew's novels feature similar sassy characters and snappy dialogue that Cabot readers may enjoy. Her most recent novel, *Deep Dish,* is the story of a cooking show star who's looking to make it big nationally but discovers that her career may be derailed by a handsome competitor.

Helen Fielding. Well known as the chick lit originator, Fielding's Bridget Jones novels are sure to appeal to Cabot fans, particularly those who enjoy Cabot's epistolary novels, *The Boy Next Door, Boy Meets Girl,* and *Every Boy's Got One.*

Marian Keyes.   Several of Keyes's chick lit novels, notably *Watermelon,* share the same sense of wry humor that Cabot readers appreciate. Some of her later novels get into darker themes, but Cabot readers should also enjoy Keyes's essay collections, *Under the Duvet, Further under the Duvet,* and *Cracks in My Foundation.*

Sophie Kinsella. Kinsella's Shopaholic series (*Confessions of a Shopaholic, Shopaholic Takes Manhattan, Shopaholic Ties the Knot, Shopaholic and Sister, Shopaholic and Baby*) are sure bets for Cabot fans, as they are similar in pace, humor, and fluff factor.

Elizabeth Cadell (1903–1989)
Family Stories; Saga
Biographical Sketch

Violet Elizabeth Cadell was born into a colonial military family on November 10, 1903, in Calcutta, India. As Elizabeth Cadell, she is known for writing gentle romantic family stories, often set in Spain and Portugal. She also used the pseudonym Harriet Ainsworth. The plots of her novels frequently involve eccentric characters and an independent heroine. She began writing in 1946, and completed 57 novels before her death on October 9, 1989.

> Decided to work at something which I could do in my own hours and discovered writing. Can recommend it to all lazy women. (Elizabeth Cadell, *Last Straw for Harriet*, 1947)

Major Works

Novels

My Dear Aunt Flora (1946)
Last Straw for Harriet (1947)
River Lodge (1948)
Gay Pursuit (1948)
Iris in Winter (1949)
Brimstone in the Garden (1950)
The Greenwood Shady (1951)
Enter Mrs. Belchamber (1951)
Men and Angels (1952)
Crystal Clear (1953)
Spring Green (1953)
The Cuckoo in Spring (1954)
Money to Burn (1954)
Around the Rugged Rock (1954)
Consider the Lilies (1955)
The Lark Shall Sing (1955)
The Blue Sky of Spring (1956)
I Love a Lass (1956)
Bridal Array (1957)
Shadows on the Water (1958)
The Green Empress (1958)
Sugar Candy Cottage (1958)
Alice, Where Art Thou? (1958)
The Yellow Brick Road (1960)
Honey for Tea (1961)

Six Impossible Things (1961)
The Toy Sword (1962)
Letter to My Love (1963)
Mixed Marriage: The Diary of a Portuguese Bride (1963)
Come Be My Guest (1964)
Canary Yellow (1965)
The Fox from His Lair (1965)
The Corner Shop (1966)
The Stratton Story (1967)
Mrs. Westerby Changes Course (1968)
The Golden Collar (1969)
The Friendly Air (1970)
The Past Tense of Love (1970)
Home for the Wedding (1971)
The Haymaker (1972)
Deck with Flowers (1973)
Royal Summons (1973)
The Fledgling (1975)
Game in Diamonds (1976)
Parson's House (1977)
The Round Dozen (1978)
River Lodge (1978)
Return Match (1979)
Family Gathering (1979)
The Marrying Kind (1980)
Any Two Can Play (1981)
A Lion in the Way (1982)
Remains to Be Seen (1983)
The Waiting Game (1985)
The Empty Nest (1986)
Out of the Nest (1987)
Out of the Rain (1987)

Research Sources

Encyclopedias and Handbooks: CA; TCRWH

Biographies and Interviews

Reynolds, Janet Cadell. *A Biography of Elizabeth Cadell.* Seymour, TN: Lady
    Grantly Publishing, 2005.

Web Sites

Elizabeth Cadell. http://www.elizabethcadell.com/. Last visited January 20,
    2008. Fan club site featuring brief biographical information, quotations,
    photographs, and bibliography.

Jennifer Chiaverini (1969–)
Gentle
Biographical Sketch

Jennifer Chiaverini was born in 1969. She has taught writing at Pennsylvania State University. An avid quilter, she started writing fiction about a quilting club, *The Elm Creek Quilters* in 1999.

Chiaverini's gentle, heartwarming novels revolve around the women of Elm Creek Manor, Pennsylvania, who become friends despite their different backgrounds and personalities. She lives in Madison, Wisconsin, where she also designs a line of quilting fabrics for Red Rooster Fabrics.

> Young writers are often advised to "write what you know," and since I knew about quilters their quirks, their inside jokes, their quarrels and kindnesses—the lives of quilters became a natural subject for me. (Jennifer Chiaverini, *Library Journal* interview, 2005)

Major Works

Novels

Elm Creek Quilts Series: *The Quilter's Apprentice* (1999), *Round Robin* (2000), *The Cross Country Quilters* (2001), *The Runaway Quilt* (2002), *The Quilter's Legacy* (2003), *The Master Quilter* (2004), *The Sugar Camp Quilt: An Elm Creek Quilts Novel* (2005), *The Christmas Quilt* (2005), *Circle of Quilters*, (2006), *The Quilter's Homecoming: An Elm Creek Quilts Novel* (2007), *The Winding Ways Quilt* (2008).

Research Sources

Encyclopedias and Handbooks: CA

Biographies and Interviews

"Cover to Cover: Jennifer Chiaverini Interview." *Flypod.* Available at http://www.trumix.com/podcast.php?mode=podshow&p=7617&s=1502331. May 3, 2007. Last visited June 27, 2008. Audio interview with Chiaverini about *The Quilters Homecoming.*

Hoffert, Barbara. "Q&A : Jennifer Chiaverini." *Library Journal.* March 15, 2005. Available online at http://www.libraryjournal.com/article/CA509615.html. Last visited July 1, 2008.

"Jennifer Chiaverini: The Quilter's Homecoming." *Simon and Schuster.* Available at http://video.aol.com/video-detail/jennifer-chiaverini-the-quilters-homecoming/9055888. Last visited June 27, 2008. Video interview with Chiaverini about the art of quiltmaking.

Criticism and Readers' Guides

Reader's guide for The *Quilter's Legacy. Penguin.* http://us.penguingroup. com/static/rguides/us/quilters_legacy.html. Last visited June 27, 2008.

Reading group guide for *The Quilter's Apprentice Reading Group Guides.* http://www.readinggroupguides.com/guides_Q/quilters_apprentice1.asp. Last visited June 27, 2008.

Web Sites

Ewing, Jody. "'Quilt' Stitches Ties to Underground Railroad." *Jody Ewing. com.* Last visited June 27, 2008. http://www.jodyewing.com/jennifer_chia verini_04_02.html 04/25/02.

Jennifer Chiaverini Official Web Site. http://www.elmcreek.net. Last visited June 27, 2008. Features bibliography, gallery of quilts, and FAQ section.

Pearl Cleage (1948–)
African American; Mainstream
Biographical Sketch

Pearl Cleage was born on December 7, 1948, in Springfield, Massachusetts. An acclaimed playwright and poet, she also writes women's fiction featuring strong African American women, social issues, and family/community relationships. Her first novel, *What Looks Like Crazy on an Ordinary Day,* was an Oprah's Book Club selection and won the Black Caucus of the American Library Association Literary Award in 1998. She lives in Atlanta, Georgia.

> I hope that working in a number of forms brings my work and my ideas forward to the widest number of people possible. I'm sure they all influence each other and overlap in many ways. I don't think too much about that, however, outside of knowing that being a playwright influenced my decision to write my novels first person. (Pearl Cleage, *Bookreporter* interview. 2001. http://www.bookreporter.com/authors/au-cleage-pearl. asp. Last visited June 27, 2008)

Major Works

Novels

What Looks Like Crazy on an Ordinary Day (1997)
I Wish I Had a Red Dress (2001)
Some Things I Never Thought I'd Do (2003)
Babylon Sisters (2005)
Baby Brother's Blues (2006)
Seen it All and Done the Rest (2008)

Research Sources

Encyclopedias and Handbooks: CA

"Pearl Cleage," in *Dictionary of Literary Biography, Volume 228: Twentieth-Century American Dramatists, Second Series*. Detroit, MI: Gale, 2000. pp. 53–58.

Biographies and Interviews

Chideya, Farai. "Playwright and Novelist Pearl Cleage." *NPR News and Notes.* August 15, 2005. http://www.npr.org/templates/story/story.php?storyId=4800216. Last visited June 27, 2008. Audio interview clip.

"Pearl Cleage." *African American Literature Book Club.* http://aalbc.com/authors/cleagepearl.htm. Last visited June 27, 2008.

"Pearl Cleage." *Bookreporter.com.* http://www.bookreporter.com/authors/aucleage-pearl.asp. Last visited June 27, 2008.

"Pearl Cleage." *New Georgia Encyclopedia.* February 13, 2006. http://www.georgiaencyclopedia.org/nge/Article.jsp?id=h-2564. Last visited June 27, 2008.

"3 R's." *The Paula Gordon Show.* http://www.paulagordon.com/shows/cleage/. August 23, 2004. Last visited June 27, 2008. Radio interview with Cleage.

Weiss, Hedy. "Lifelong Interest Inspires Playwright." *Chicago Sun-Times,* March 15, 1998, p. 13.

Criticism and Readers' Guides

Reading group guide for *I Wish I Had a Red Dress. Reading Group Guides.* http://www.readinggroupguides.com/guides3/i_wish_i_had_a_red_dress2.asp. Last visited June 27, 2008.

Reading group guide for *What Looks Like Crazy on an Ordinary Day. Reading Group Guides.* http://www.readinggroupguides.com/guides3/what_looks_like_crazy1.asp. Last visited June 27, 2008.

Web Sites

Pearl Cleage Official Web Site. http://www.pearlcleage.net/. Last visited June 27, 2008. Features photo gallery and bibliography.

Jackie Collins (1937–)
Glitz and Glamour

Biographical Sketch

Jackie Collins was born on October 4, 1937, in London, England. She is the sister of actress Joan Collins. She began writing racy stories in high school that she would sell to her classmates. Her novels are known for their lavish settings; over-the-top glamorous characters seeking money and power, drugs, violence; and steamy sex scenes. Several of her novels have been adapted as television movies. She currently lives in Los Angeles, California.

> If you're a true storyteller, you tell stories about the people and events around you. I was raised in a show-business family, so I was never in awe of famous people, and I decided they were the perfect subjects for me to write about. (Jackie Collins, *CNN online chat*, 2000. http://www. cnn.com/chat/transcripts/2000/10/16/collins/index.html. Last visited January 20, 2008)

Major Works

Novels

The World Is Full of Married Men (1968)
The Stud (1970)
The World Is Full of Divorced Women (1975)
Lovers and Gamblers (1978)
The Bitch (1979)
Chances (1981)
Hollywood Wives (1983)
Sinners (1984)
Lucky (1985)
Hollywood Husbands (1986)
Rock Star (1988)
Lady Boss (1990)
American Star: A Love Story (1993)
Hollywood Kids (1994)
Vendetta: Lucky's Revenge (1996)
Thrill! (1997)
Dangerous Kiss (1999)
Lethal Seduction (2000)
Hollywood Wives: The New Generation (2001)
Deadly Embrace (2002)
Hollywood Divorces (2003)
Lovers and Players (2006)
Drop Dead Beautiful (2007)

Research Sources

Encyclopedias and Handbooks: CA

Biographies and Interviews. Ascher-Walsh, Rebecca. "L.A. Confidential: Once Again, Novelist Jackie Collins Dives Into The Steamy Love Lives of

Hollywood's Beautiful People." *Entertainment Weekly.* August 3, 2001 Available online at http://www.ew.com/ew/article/0,,255428,00.html. Last visited May 16, 2008.

"Chat With Jackie Collins." *CNN Online.* October 16, 2000. http://www.cnn.com/chat/transcripts/2000/10/16/collins/index.html. Last visited January 20, 2008.

"Interview with Jackie Collins." *MSNBC Interactive.* June 26, 2007. http://today.msnbc.msn.com/id/19437399/. Last visited January 20, 2008.

"Jackie Collins' Home: Take a Tour with the Author." *Lifetime TV Network.* http://videos.mylifetime.com/?fr_story=FRTHEBRAIN202342&rf=sitemap. Last visited May 16, 2008. Features a video tour of Collin's lavish home, aired on Lifetime TV Network.

Web Sites

"Jackie Collins." *Simon and Schuster.* http://www.simonsays.com/content/destination.cfm?sid=33&pid=341081 Last visited January 20, 2008. Publisher's Web site.

Jackie Collins Official Website. http://www.jackiecollins.com Last visited January 20, 2008. Author's official Web site.

If You Like Jackie Collins

Collins is known for over-the-top glitz and glamour. The lifestyles of the rich and famous are in full display in her novels, which usually feature plenty of steamy sex and soap opera level drama as well.

Then You Might Like

Olivia Goldsmith. Many of Goldsmith's novels are set in the glamorous worlds of television, book publishing, and fashion. Her novel *Flavor of the Month* is the story of three rising television starlets, each of who has a secret she would die to protect—and one of them does.

Judith Krantz. Krantz's rags-to-riches soap opera plots feature dazzling settings and characters in high-powered occupations. They are fast-paced stories of women struggling to get to the top, usually by any means necessary.

Danielle Steel. Steel is less gritty and dramatic than Collins, but her novels are packed with colorful characters, subplots, and details that will appeal to those who like the "overstuffed" feel of a Collins novel.

Penny Vincenzi. Vincenzi's glitzy novels cover the jet-setting lives of glamorous women and their high-powered families. Wildly popular in Britain, she is a good match for Collins fans, as her stories brim with soap opera level drama.

Claire Cook (1955–)
Light; Women's Romantic Fiction
Biographical Sketch

Claire Cook was born 1955, in Alexandria, Virginia. She graduated magna cum laude from Syracuse University, majoring in film and creative writing. She worked as a Montessori teacher, a landscape designer, and a choreographer before publishing her first novel in her forties.

Her novels, light-hearted and humorous, often feature quirky families and romantic relationships. She is a member of the Cape Cod Writers Center faculty and lives in Scituate, Massachusetts.

> For me it's all about the characters. I'm always surprised when I read, "Claire Cook writes about relationships" or "suburbia" or "transitions" or "family," because I thought I was writing about Ginger and Geri and all the rest of them. (Claire Cook, *Fresh Fiction* interview, 2007. http://freshfiction.com/page.php?id=440. Last visited June 27, 2008)

Major Works

Novels

Ready to Fall (2000)
Must Love Dogs (2002)
Multiple Choice (2004)
Life's a Beach (2007)
Summer Blowout (2008)

Research Sources

Encyclopedias and Handbooks: CA

Biographies and Interviews

"Claire Cook." *Barnes & Noble Meet the Writers.* http://www.barnesandnoble.com/writers/writer.asp?cid=1022602. Last visited June 27, 2008.
Vido, Jennifer. *Fresh Fiction.* June 5, 2007. http://freshfiction.com/page.php?id=440. Last visited June 27, 2008.

Criticism and Readers' Guides

Reader's guide for *Multiple Choice. Penguin.* http://us.penguingroup.com/static/rguides/us/multiple_choice.html. Last visited June 27, 2008.
Reading guide for *Life's a Beach. Hyperion.* http://www.hyperionbooks.com/readingguide.asp?ISBN=1401303242. Last visited June 27, 2008.

Web Sites

Claire Cook Official Web Site. http://www.clairecook.com/. Last visited June 27, 2008. Features blog, photo gallery, and newsletter.
"Summer Blowout." *ClaireCookNovelist.* Available at http://www.youtube.com/watch?v=NzNZlYeqhMs. Last visited June 27, 2008. Video clip of Cook reading from her novel, *Summer Blowout.*

Catherine Cookson (1906–1998)
Historical; Saga; Women's Romantic Fiction
Biographical Sketch

Catherine Cookson was born on June 20, 1906, in Tyne Dock, South Shields, England. She had a difficult childhood, living in poverty and never knowing her father. Suffering from a rare blood disease, she was unable to have children, which caused a struggle with depression. Her husband suggested she start writing to work through her sadness, and she published her first novel, *Kate Hannigan* in 1950. One of Britain's most beloved and most prolific authors, Cookson wrote nearly 100 novels in her lifetime and was also a respected children's author. Her novels feature northern English settings and strong female characters, usually struggling with British class differences. Many of her novels have been made into television movies. Cookson also published three books under the pseudonym Catherine Marchant.

Cookson was awarded an OBE in 1985 and was made a Dame in 1993. She died on June 11, 1998, in England. Several novels, which she had dictated from her sickbed, were published posthumously.

> The madness was strong on me the day I received a letter, through my agent, asking if I would go to London and have lunch with my publisher. He was no longer *the* publisher, he was *my* publisher. It was a wonderful feeling to have a publisher. (Catherine Cookson, *Our Kate: An Autobiography.* Indianapolis: Bobbs-Merrill, 1971)

Major Works

Novels

The Hamilton series: *Hamilton* (1983), *Goodbye Hamilton* (1984), *Harold* (1985)
The Kate Hannigan series: *Kate Hannigan* (1950), *Kate Hannigan's Girl* (2001)
The Tilly Trotter Trilogy: *Tilly Trotter* (1980), *Tilly Trotter Wed* (1981), *Tilly Trotter Widowed* (1982)

The Mallen Trilogy: *The Mallen Girl* (1973), *The Mallen Streak* (1973), *The Mallen Litter* (1974)

The Bill Bailey Trilogy: *Bill Bailey* (1986), *Bill Bailey's Lot* (1987), *Bill Bailey's Daughter* (1988)

The Mary Ann Stories: *A Grand Man* (1954), *The Lord and Mary Ann* (1956), *The Devil and Mary Ann* (1958), *Love and Mary Ann* (1961), *Life and Mary Ann* (1962), *Marriage and Mary Ann* (1964), *Mary Ann's Angels* (1965), *Mary Ann and Bill* (1967)

The Fifteen Streets (1952)

Colour Blind (1953)

Maggie Rowan (1954)

Rooney (1957)

The Menagerie (1958)

Fanny McBride (1959)

Fenwick Houses (1960)

The Garment (1962)

The Blind Miller (1963)

The Wingless Bird (1964)

Hannah Massey (1964)

The Long Corridor (1965)

The Unbaited Trap (1966)

Slinky Jane (1967)

Katie Mulholland (1967)

The Round Tower (1968)

The Husband (1969)

The Nice Bloke (1969)

The Glass Virgin (1969)

The Invitation (1970)

The Dwelling Place (1971)

Feathers in the Fire (1971)

Pure as the Lily (1972)

The Invisible Cord (1975)

The Gambling Man (1975)

The Tide of Life (1976)

The Girl (1977)

The Cinder Path (1978)

The Man Who Cried (1979)

The Whip (1983)

The Black Velvet Gown (1984)

A Dinner of Herbs (1985)

The Bannaman Legacy (1985)

The Moth (1986)

The Parson's Daughter (1987)

The Harrogate Secret (1988)
The Cultured Handmaiden (1988)
The Black Candle (1989)
The Gillyvors (1990)
My Beloved Son (1991)
The Rag Nymph (1991)
The House of Women (1992)
The Maltese Angel (1992)
The Golden Straw (1993)
The Forester Girl (1993)
The Year of the Virgins (1993)
The Tinker's Girl (1995)
Justice Is a Woman (1995)
The Bonny Dawn (1996)
The Obsession (1997)
The Upstart (1998)
The Blind Years (1998)
Riley (1998)
Solace of Sin (1998)
The Desert Crop (1999)
The Thursday Friend (1999)
My Land of the North (1999)
Desert Crop (1999)
A House Divided (2000)
Rosie of the River (2000)
Silent Lady (2002)

Other Works of Interest

Let Me Make Myself Plain: A Personal Anthology. London: Bantam, 1988.
Our Kate: An Autobiography. Indianapolis: Bobbs-Merrill, 1971.

Research Sources

Encyclopedias and Handbooks: CA; TCRHW

Biographies and Interviews

Dudgeon, Piers. *Kate's Daughter: The Real Catherine Cookson.* London: Bantam, 2003.
Goodwin, Cliff. *To Be a Lady: The Story of Catherine Cookson.* London: Century, 1994.
Jones, Kathleen. *Catherine Cookson: The Biography.* London: Constable, 1999.

Web Sites

"Catherine Cookson." *Exclusive Books.* http://www.exclusivebooks.com/
    features/authors/ccookson.php?PHPSESSID=PHPSESSID. Last visited
    May 16, 2008.
"Catherine Cookson." *Simon and Schuster.* Publisher Web site. http://www.
    simonsays.com/content/destination.cfm?tab=1&pid=328489. Last visited
    January 20, 2008.

Barbara Delinsky (1945–)
Issue Driven; Women's Romantic Fiction
Biographical Sketch

Barbara Delinsky was born on August 9, 1945, in Boston, Massachusetts.
After earning a BA in Psychology from Tufts University and an MA in Soci-
ology from Boston College, she worked as a researcher for the Massachusetts
Society for the Prevention of Cruelty to Children; and also as a newspaper
photographer and reporter. When Delinsky was eight years old, her mother
died from breast cancer; and Delinsky is a breast cancer survivor herself.

She began writing paperback romances, and shifted into more character-
driven and issue-driven novels with the publication of her 1994 novel, *For
My Daughters.* Delinsky runs a charitable foundation, funding an ongoing
research fellowship at Massachusetts General Hospital. She lives in Newton,
Massachusetts.

> I gradually gave emotional elements such as family crises, sibling ri-
> valry, and friendship more time on stage and the romance less. I worked
> hard—still do—on making my writing more efficient and sophisticated.
> The greatest obstacle to overcome? Changing the way booksellers per-
> ceive me. To this day, much of the public thinks I'm still a romance
> writer, when, in fact, I haven't written a romance in over ten years!
> (Barbara Delinsky, *Writers Write* interview. http://www.writerswrite.
> com/journal/jun00/delinsky.htm. Last visited June 27, 2008)

Major Works

Novels

Finger Prints (1984)
Within Reach (1986)
Twilight Whispers (1987)
Commitments (1988)
Heart of the Night (1989)
A Woman Betrayed (1992)

The Passions of Chelsea Kane (1992)
Suddenly (1993)
More than Friends (1993)
Outsider (1993)
For My Daughters (1994)
Together Alone (1995)
Shades of Grace (1995)
A Woman's Place (1997)
Three Wishes (1997)
Coast Road (1998)
Rekindled (1998)
Lake News (1999)
The Vineyard (2000)
The Woman Next Door (2001)
An Accidental Woman (2002)
Flirting with Pete (2003)
The Summer I Dared (2004)
Looking for Peyton Place (2005)
Family Tree (2006)
The Secret Between Us (2008)

Research Sources

Encyclopedias and Handbooks: CA

Biographies and Interviews

"Barbara Delinsky." *Barnes and Noble Meet the Writers.* http://www.barne sandnoble.com/writers/writer.asp?cid=883221. Last visited June 26, 2008.

"Barbara Delinsky." *BookWrap Central.* http://www.bookwrapcentral.com/ authors/barbaradelinsky.htm. Last visited June 27, 2008. Video interview.

"Meet the Author: Barbara Delinsky." *BookPage.* July 1999. http://www.book page.com/9907bp/barbara_delinsky.html. Last visited June 27, 2008.

Vido, Jennifer. "Interview with Barbara Delinsky." *Fresh Fiction.* http://fresh fiction.com/page.php?id=814. Last visited June 26, 2008.

White, Claire E. "A Conversation with Barbara Delinsky." *Writers Write: The Internet Writing Journal.* Last visited June 26, 2008. http://www.writers write.com/journal/jun00/delinsky.htm

Criticism and Readers' Guides

Reading group guide for *Family Tree. Reading Group Guides.* http://www. readinggroupguides.com/guides3/family_tree1.asp. Last visited June 27, 2008.

Reading group guide for *Flirting with Pete. Reading Group Guides.* http://
www.readinggroupguides.com/guides3/flirting_with_pete1.asp. Last visited June 27, 2008.

Web Sites

"Barbara Delinsky." *Goodreads.* http://www.goodreads.com/author/show/
36492.Barbara_Delinsky. Last visited June 27, 2008. Author's official page
on Goodreads.
"Barbara Delinsky." *Simon & Schuster.* http://www.simonsays.com/content/
destination.cfm?tab=1&pid=353589. Last visited June 27, 2008. Official
publisher Web site.
Barbara Delinsky Official Web Site. http://www.barbaradelinsky.com/. Last
visited June 27, 2008. Features author's blog, brief biography, and podcasts.
"Breast Cancer Awareness Author Roundtable" *Authors On The Web.* http://
www.Authorsontheweb.com/features/0110-breast-cancer/0110-BCAM.
asp. Last visited June 27, 2008.

Katie Fforde (1952–)
Light; Women's Romantic Fiction
Biographical Sketch

Katie Fforde was born on September 27, 1952, in Wimbledon, England.
For 10 years she attempted to write paperback romances, before turning
to contemporary women's fiction and successfully getting published in her
40s. She writes light, contemporary novels about average women in England
and their families and relationships. There is usually a gentle romance in her
novels.

Fforde is the cousin of fantasy novelist Jasper Fforde. She lives in Stroud,
Gloucestershire, England.

I do have fun writing my books but although I do feel terribly lucky
earning my living from something I enjoy, it does feel like real work,
especially now I am getting published. The most fun I had writing was
when I was trying to write for Mills and Boon. I was eternally optimistic
about getting published (wrongly!) and I had friends doing the same
thing. We would get together and moan about our latest rejection letters. It seems more serious now. (Katie Fforde, http://www.prairieden.
com/front_porch/visiting_authors/fforde.html. Last visited June 26,
2008)

Major Works

Novels

Living Dangerously (1995)
The Rose Revived (1996)
Stately Pursuits (1997)
Wild Designs (1997)
Life Skills (1999)
Thyme Out (2000)
Second Thyme Around (2001)
Highland Fling (2002)
Artistic License (2002)
Paradise Fields (2004)
Restoring Grace (2006)
Bidding for Love (2007)

Research Sources

Encyclopedias and Handbooks: CA

Biographies and Interviews

Bolton, Kathleen. "Author Interview: Katie Fforde." *Writer Unboxed.* February 22, 2008. http://writerunboxed.com/2008/02/19/author-interview-katie-fforde/. Last visited June 26, 2008.

Hussain, Ali. "Fame and Fortune: Katie Fforde." *The Times Online (UK).* June 22, 2008. http://business.timesonline.co.uk/tol/business/money/article 4187217.ece. Last visited June 26, 2008.

"Katie Fforde." *Meet the Author.* http://www.meettheauthor.co.uk/bookbites/576.html. Last visited June 26, 2008. Audio interview clip.

Warwick, Nicola. "Katie Fforde." *Prairie Den.* http://www.prairieden.com/front_porch/visiting_authors/fforde.html. Last visited June 26, 2008.

Criticism and Readers' Guides

Reading guide for *Thyme Out. Random House UK.* http://www.randomhouse.co.uk/readersgroup/readingguide.htm?command=Search&db=/catalog/main.txt&eqisbndata=0099280248. Last visited June 26, 2008.

Web Sites

"Katie Fforde 'Bedside': The Book Show Episode 13." *The Book Show.* Available online at http://www.youtube.com/watch?v=SqXqLZAN_ms&feature=related. Last visited June 26, 2008. Video clip of Fforde talking about the books on her bedside.

Katie Fforde Official Web Site. http://www.katiefforde.com/. Last visited June 26, 2008. Features U.S. and U.K. book lists, translation of British slang, and author essays.

Helen Fielding (1958–)
Chick Lit; Humorous
Biographical Sketch

Helen Fielding was born on February 19, 1958, in Morley, West Yorkshire, England. She attended Oxford University and was a producer for BBC-TV and columnist for the London *Independent* before writing her first novel, *Cause Celeb,* in 1994. However, her 1997 novel *Bridget Jones's Diary* was her breakout work, and kicked off the chick lit phenomenon.

A film version of *Bridget Jones's Diary* was released in 2001, and the film version of *Bridget Jones: The Edge of Reason* was released in 2004. Fielding lives in London, England.

My books have all generated controversy. Bridget Jones was considered a disgrace to feminism. Comedy tends to come out of things which are quite painful and serious. (Helen Fielding, *Time* interview, 2004. http://www.time.com/time/magazine/article/0,9171,646371,00.html. Last visited June 27, 2008)

Major Works

Novels

Bridget Jones's Diary (1998)
Bridget Jones: The Edge of Reason (2000)
Bridget Jones's Guide to Life (2001)
Cause Celeb (2001; first published in the United Kingdom in 1994)
Olivia Joules and the Overactive Imagination (2004)

Research Sources

Encyclopedias and Handbooks: CA; CLC

"Helen Fielding," in *Dictionary of Literary Biography, Volume 231: British Novelists Since 1960, Fourth Series.* Detroit, MI: Gale, 2000. pp. 106–111.

Biographies and Interviews

"Author Helen Fielding." *Time.* June 16, 1998. http://www.time.com/time/community/transcripts/chattr061698.html. Last visited June 27, 2008. Online chat transcript

Daum, Meghan. "Keeping Up with Ms. Jones," *Village Voice.* June 30, 1998. Available online at http://bridgetarchive.altervista.org/bjd_keeping_up. htm. Last visited June 27, 2008.

"Helen Fielding." *The Guardian (UK).* http://books.guardian.co.uk/authors/ author/0„-203,00.html. Last visited June 27, 2008.

Weich, Dave. "Helen Fielding is not Bridget Jones." *Powells.* http://www.pow ells.com/authors/fielding.html. Last visited June 27, 2008.

Winters, Rebecca. "Q&A With Helen Fielding." *Time.* June 6, 2004. Available online at http://www.time.com/time/magazine/article/0,9171,646371,00. html. Last visited June 27, 2008.

Criticism and Readers' Guides

"Helen Fielding: She's Back—(Hurrah!)." *The Independent.* July 31, 2005. http://www.independent.co.uk/news/people/helen-fielding-shes-back-hurrah-500875.html. Last visited June 27, 2008.

Marsh, Kelly A. "Contextualizing Bridget Jones." *College Literature* (31:1) 2004, 52–72.

Reading guide for *Bridget Jones' Diary. Penguin.* http://us.penguingroup. com/static/rguides/us/bridget_joness_diary.html. Last visited June 27, 2008.

Web Sites

Bridget Jones Online Archive. http://bridgetarchive.altervista.org/. Last visited June 27, 2008.

"Helen Fielding's To-Read List." *O, the Oprah Magazine* June 2004. http:// www.oprah.com/obc/omag/obc_omag_200406_books.jhtml. Last visited June 27, 2008.

Joy Fielding (1945–)
Issue Driven; Romantic Suspense
Biographical Sketch

Joy Fielding was born on March 18, 1945, in Toronto, Canada. After a brief acting career in the late 1960s as Joy Tepperman, she became a novelist and published her first book, *Best of Friends* in 1972. Her novel *See Jane Run* was made into a television movie in 1995, and *The Other Woman* was made into a television movie in 2008.

Fielding writes in a variety of styles, from romantic suspense to tearjerker issue-driven novels. They all revolve around ordinary women dealing with extraordinary circumstances; and focus on complex issues such as divorce, child abductions, abusive relationships, and fatal illnesses. Fielding lives in Toronto, Canada, and Palm Beach, Florida.

I love writing because it's the only time in my life when I feel I have complete control. Nobody does or says anything I don't tell them to—although even this amount of control is illusory because there comes a point where the characters take over and tell you what they think they should say and do. (Joy Fielding, http://www.joyfielding.com/v2/biography.htm. Last visited June 26, 2008)

Major Works

Novels

The Best of Friends (1972)
The Transformation (1976)
Trance (1979)
Kiss Mommy Goodbye (1981)
The Other Woman (1983)
Life Penalty (1984)
The Deep End (1986)
Good Intentions (1989)
See Jane Run (1991)
Tell Me No Secrets (1993)
Don't Cry Now (1995)
Missing Pieces (1997)
The First Time (2000)
Grand Avenue (2001)
Whispers and Lies (2002)
Lost (2003)
Puppet (2005)
Mad River Road (2006)
Heartstopper (2007)
Charley's Web (2008)

Research Sources

Encyclopedias and Handbooks: CA

Biographies and Interviews

Bay, Kinda. "Bestselling Author Joy Fielding." *A 'n' E Vibe.* http://www.anevibe.com/books/bestselling-author-joy-fielding.html. Last visited March 6, 2009.
"Joy Fielding." *Bill Thompson's Eye on Books.* http://www.eyeonbooks.com/iap.php?authID=557. Last visited June 26, 2008. Audio interview clip.
"Joy Fielding on *Charley's Web.*" *BookLounge.* Available at http://www.youtube.com/watch?v=CbtD11XEJmo. Last visited June 26, 2008. Video interview clip.

Jung, Cherie. "Interview of Joy Fielding." *Over My Dead Body*. 1995. http://www.overmydeadbody.com/fielding.htm. Last visited June 26, 2008.

MacDonald, Jay. "Fame & Fortune: Author Joy Fielding." *Bankrate*. July 28, 2007. http://www.bankrate.com/brm/news/investing/20070728_fame_fortune_joy_fielding_a1.asp. Last visited June 26, 2008.

Richards, Linda. "Joy Fielding." *January Magazine*. October 2001. http://januarymagazine.com/profiles/fielding.html. Last visited June 26, 2008.

Wagner, Vit. "Joy Fielding Okay with Being 'Popular.'" *Toronto Star*. March 28, 2008. Available online at http://www.thestar.com/comment/columnists/article/404695. Last visited June 26, 2008.

Web Sites

Joy Fielding Official Web Site. http://www.joyfielding.com. Last visited June 26, 2008. Features biography, book list, and photo album.

Fannie Flagg (1941–)
Gentle; Humorous

Biographical Sketch

Fannie Flagg was born Patricia Neal on September 21, 1941, in Birmingham, Alabama. She attended the University of Alabama, and had a successful career as an actress and television writer, best known for her work on *Candid Camera,* before turning to novel writing. Since there was already an American actress by the name of Patricia Neal, she changed her name to Fannie Flagg. In addition to her novels, she has produced four comedy albums.

Flagg's novels are set in the South, usually in small towns full of eccentric characters. She uses folksy dialogue and gentle humor in her books, and often portrays strong women who exceed societal expectations. Her novel *Fried Green Tomatoes at the Whistle Stop Café* was made into a successful movie in 1991, and Flagg was nominated for an Academy Award for the screenplay. Flagg lives in Santa Barbara, California, and New York City.

[After learning she was called "The Most Sentimental Writer in America"] I thought, isn't that fabulous? And my friends said, "No, Fannie, that's not good." But it is. The easiest thing in the world is to be smart-alecky and cynical and snide and jaded. It's hard to keep your heart open. (Fannie Flagg, *BookPage* interview. http://www.bookpage.com/0208bp/fannie_flag.html. Last visited June 27, 2008)

Major Works

Novels

Coming Attractions: A Wonderful Novel (1981), re-published as *Daisy Fay and the Miracle Man,* (1992)
Fried Green Tomatoes at the Whistle Stop Café (1987)
Welcome to the World, Baby Girl!: A Novel (1998)
Standing in the Rainbow (2002)
A Redbird Christmas (2004)
Can't Wait to Get to Heaven (2006)

Research Sources

Encyclopedias and Handbooks: CA

Biographies and Interviews

"Fannie Flagg." *Barnes and Noble Meet the Writers.* http://www.barnesand noble.com/writers/writer.asp?cid=64794. Last visited June 26, 2008.
"Fannie Flagg." *BookReporter.com.* http://www.bookreporter.com/authors/ au-flagg-fannie.asp. Last visited June 26, 2008.
Kanner, Ellen. "Still Young at Heart: Fannie Flagg Rewrites Her Lonely Child hood." *BookPage.* August 2002. http://www.bookpage.com/0208bp/fan nie_flag.html. Last visited June 26, 2008.
Wired For Books. "Audio interview with Dan Swain." 1987. http://wiredforbooks. org/fannieflagg/index.htm. Last visited June 26, 2008.

Criticism and Readers' Guides

Dunne, Michael. "Bakhtin Eats Some Fried Green Tomatoes: Dialogic Ele ments in Fannie Flagg's Famous Novel." *Studies in Popular Culture* (28:1) 2005, 25–36.
Reading group guide for *Fried Green Tomatoes. Reading Group Guides.* http:// www.readinggroupguides.com/guides_F/fried_green_tomatoes1.asp. Last visited June 26, 2008.

Web Sites

"Fannie Flagg." *MySpace.com.* http://profile.myspace.com/index.cfm?fuseac tion=user.viewprofile&friendID=99188215. Last visited June 26, 2008. Author's official MySpace page.
"Fannie Flagg." *Random House.* http://www.randomhouse.com/features/fan nieflagg/. Last visited June 26, 2008. Official publisher Web site.
Whistle Stop Café. http://www.whistlestopcafe.com/index.html. Last visited June 26, 2008. Official Web site of the actual Whistle Stop Café in Irondale, Alabama.

If You Like Fannie Flagg

Fannie Flagg is a great storyteller with a gentle sense of humor. Her novels, set in the South, feature small towns full of eccentric characters.

Then You Might Like

Maeve Binchy. While Binchy does not have quite the same sense of humor as Flagg, readers who enjoy small-town settings with folksy characters will enjoy some of Binchy's novels, such as *Whitethorn Woods,* the story of a town dealing with an impending highway cutting through it, or *Evening Class,* which follows a diverse group students in an Italian language course.

Cassandra King. King's novels feature strong Southern women and are full of friendships, family relationships, and fun, often eccentric characters.

Ann B. Ross. Ross's Miss Julia novels (*Miss Julia Speaks Her Mind, Miss Julia Takes Over,* et al.) will offer Flagg's fans a familiar small-town setting, eccentric Southern characters, and gentle humor.

Haywood Smith. Smith writes humorous fiction about sassy, older women. Her Red Hat Trilogy (*The Red Hat Club, The Red Hat Club Rides Again, Wedding Belle*) will appeal to those who enjoy Flagg's sassy, mature characters.

Adriana Trigiani. Trigiani's Big Stone Gap novels (*Big Stone Gap, Big Cherry Holler, Milk Glass Moon, Home to Big Stone Gap*) offer the same small-town, gossipy appeal with warm and familiar characters that Flagg's novels do.

Dorothea Benton Frank
Mainstream
Biographical Sketch

Dorothea Benton Frank was born in Sullivan's Island, South Carolina. She began writing in her forties after the death of her mother, as a way to process her grief. She also wanted to earn enough money to purchase her mother's home. Prior to that, she worked fundraising for arts and education ventures in New York and New Jersey.

Her novels take place in the coastal towns of South Carolina, and feature everyday women in realistic situations, often dealing with family and friends. She currently lives in South Carolina and New Jersey.

> Yes, writers owe their readers a huge debt. I think of my readers as my best friends whom I would never knowingly hoodwink. I try to the best of my abilities, given the constraints of life's happenings and my publisher's schedule, to give my most sincere efforts to my writing each and every day. (Dorothea Benton Frank, *Bookpleasures.com* interview.

http://www.bookpleasures.com/Lore2/idx/0/3425/article/Meet_New_
York_Times_BestSelling_Author_Dorothea_Benton_Frank.html. Last
visited June 26, 2008)

Major Works

Novels

Sullivan's Island: A Lowcountry Tale (1999)
Plantation: A Lowcountry Tale (2001)
Isle of Palms: A Lowcountry Tale (2003)
Shem Creek: A Lowcountry Tale (2004)
Pawleys Island: A Lowcountry Tale (2005)
Full of Grace (2006)
The Land of Mango Sunset (2007)
The Christmas Pearl (2007)
Bulls Island (2008)

Research Sources

Encyclopedias and Handbooks: CA

Biographies and Interviews

"Dorothea Benton Frank." *Barnes and Noble Meet the Writers.* http://www.
    barnesandnoble.com/writers/writer.asp?cid=1022193. Last visited June 27,
    2008. Features audio interview.
Hamilton, Lynn. "Frankly Speaking." *BookPage.* April 2007. http://www.
    bookpage.com/0704bp/dorothea_benton_frank.html. Last visited June 26,
    2008.
Goldman, Norm. "Meet New York Times Best-Selling Author Dorothea
    Benton Frank." March 19, 2008. *Bookpleasures.com.* http://www.book
    pleasures.com/Lore2/idx/0/3425/article/Meet_New_York_Times_BestSell
    ing_Author_Dorothea_Benton_Frank.html. Last visited June 26, 2008.
"Guest Interview: Dorothea Benton Frank." *Southern Authors Blog.* March 28,
    2008. http://southernauthors.blogspot.com/2008/03/guest-interview-dor
    othea-benton-frank.html. Last visited June 26, 2008.
Holstine, Lesa. "Interview with Dorothea Benton Frank." *Lesa's Book Cri-
    tiques.* April 27, 2008. http://lesasbookcritiques.blogspot.com/2008/04/
    interview-with-dorothea-benton-frank.html. Last visited June 26, 2008.
Stovall, Teressa. "Writing From the Heart: The Lowcountry Wit and Wisdom
    of Dorothea Benton Frank." *Montclair Times.* May 23, 2007.
Vido, Jennifer. "Fresh Fiction Interview with Dorothea Benton Frank." *Fresh
    Fiction.* December 1, 2007. http://freshfiction.com/page.php?id=666. Last
    visited June 26, 2008.

Zacharias, Karen Spears. "Interviews Dorothea Benton Frank." *Authors Round the South.* December 3, 2007. http://www.authorsroundthesouth. com/index.php/author-2-author/38-author-news-a-interviews/337- karen-spears-zacharias-interviews-dorothea-benton-frank. Last visited May 22, 2008.

Criticism and Readers' Guides

Reading group guide for *Bulls Island. Reading Group Guides.* http://www.read inggroupguides.com/guides_B/bulls_island1.asp. Last visited June 26, 2008.

Reading group guide for *Sullivan's Island. Reading Group Guides.* http:// us.penguingroup.com/static/rguides/us/sullivans_island.html. Last visited June 26, 2008.

Web Sites

"Dorothea Benton Frank." *GoodReads.* http://www.goodreads.com/author/ show/36935. Last visited June 27, 2008. Author's official page on Good reads.

"Dorothea Benton Frank." *HarperCollins.* http://www.harpercollins.com/ authors/30637/Dorothea_Benton_Frank/index.aspx. Last visited June 26, 2008. Official publisher web site.

"Dorothea Benton Frank discusses *Bulls Island* and the CCL." *Conservation League.* http://youtube.com/watch?v=VqKbxZGEDQg. Last visited June 26, 2008. Video of author discussing her book *Bulls Island.*

Dorothea Benton Frank Official Web Site. http://www.dotfrank.com. Last visited June 26, 2008. Features brief biography, recipes, and "Lowcountry Links."

If You Like Dorothea Benton Frank

Dorothea Benton Frank's novels take place in the Low Country coastal towns of South Carolina, and feature independent, everyday women in realistic situations, often dealing with family and friends.

Then You Might Like

Lois Battle. Battle's novel *Bed & Breakfast* is set in the same Low Country setting as Frank's novels, and is the story of a widow and her three grown daughters coming home trying to mend a lifetime of shattered memories.

Cassandra King. While not the same settings, King's novels feature strong Southern women and are full of friendships and family relationships, much like Frank's novels.

Jill McCorkle. McCorkle's novels feature strong Southern women, and take a close look at the way people relate to the world around them.

Mary Alice Monroe. Monroe sets her novels in the same South Carolina coastal towns as Frank, and also features women dealing with everyday trials and tribulations.

Anne Rivers Siddons. Siddons sets several of her novels in the same Low Country islands as Frank, and her novel *Low Country* is the story of the struggle between conserving natural beauty and coastal development.

Patricia Gaffney
Mainstream
Biographical Sketch

Patricia Gaffney was born in Tampa, Florida, and grew up in Bethesda, Maryland, a suburb of Washington, D.C. She taught high school for a year before becoming a freelance court reporter, before publishing her first book, a historical romance, in 1989. For the next 10 years, she wrote many paperback romances before turning to contemporary women's issues with her first hardcover release, *The Saving Graces,* in 1999.

Gaffney's women's fiction novels feature smart and mature women and the stories revolve around their friendships and family relationships. Her dialogue is clever, and the characters and situations are realistic. Patricia Gaffney currently lives in southern Pennsylvania.

> I love solitude. I think it's interesting that the majority of writers, whose job is to describe as truthfully as we can what people's lives are like, are introverts, and in fact most of us would like to be recluses. If not hermits. Two words make our hearts pound and our hands sweat: book tour. (Patricia Gaffney, *Readers Read* interview. http://www. readersread.com/features/patriciagaffney.htm. Last visited May 13, 2008)

Major Works

Novels

The Saving Graces (1999)
Circle of Three (2000)
Flight Lessons (2002)
The Goodbye Summer (2004)
Mad Dash (2007)

Research Sources

Encyclopedias and Handbooks: CA

Biographies and Interviews

"Interview with Patricia Gaffney." *Readers Read* http://www.readersread.com/
features/patriciagaffney.htm. Last visited May 13, 2008.
"Patricia Gaffney: Swimming in the Mainstream." *Crescent Blues.* http://www.
crescentblues.com/3_3issue/gaffney.shtml. Last visited May 13, 2008.

Criticism and Readers' Guides

Patricia Gaffney Official Web Site. Points of Discussion for *The Saving Graces.*
http://www.patriciagaffney.com/savinggraces_guide.html. Last visited
May 18, 2008.
Reading group guide for *Mad Dash. Random House.* http://www.random
house.com/catalog/display.pperl?isbn=9780307382115&view=rg.
Last visited May 18, 2008.

Web Sites

Patricia Gaffney Official Web Site. http://www.patriciagaffney.com/. Last vis
ited May 13, 2008. Features bibliography and "All About PG."
"Patricia Gaffney on *Circle of Three.*" *Harper Collins.* http://www.harpercol
lins.com/author/authorExtra.aspx?authorID=14270&isbn13=97800610
98369&displayType=bookessay. Last visited May 18, 2008. Brief essay
by Gaffney.

Gail Godwin (1937–)
Mainstream
Biographical Sketch

Gail Godwin was born on June 18, 1937, in Birmingham, Alabama. After
graduating from the University of North Carolina, she worked as a reporter
for the *Miami Herald.* She went back to school at the University of Iowa,
earning her M.A. degree in 1968 and her Ph.D. degree in English in 1971,
where her thesis became her first novel, *The Perfectionists.* Her novels feature
creative and intellectual women, frequently in Southern settings. She generally writes about women dealing with adversity, often in family relationships
and issues. She also writes about the creative struggle between the artist's life
and mainstream life. She has also been the librettist for several musical works
by composer Robert Starer.

Godwin is the recipient of a National Endowment for the Arts grant in
creative writing; a National Book Award nomination for *The Odd Woman;* a

Guggenheim fellowship in creative writing; American Book Awards nominations for *Violet Clay,* and for *A Mother and Two Daughters;* and an American Institute and Academy of Arts and Letters Award in Literature. She currently lives in Woodstock, New York.

> From my childhood on, librarians have anticipated my reading pleasures, learned what my passions were, suggested what to read next, and guided me when I needed a book on a certain subject but hadn't the foggiest notion of who might have written it or what it would be called. (Gail Godwin, *Bluestalking Reader* interview. http://bluestalking.type pad.com/the_bluestalking_reader/2007/03/an_interview_wi_1.html. Last visited May 18, 2008)

Major Works

Novels

The Perfectionists (1970)
Glass People (1972)
The Odd Woman (1974)
Violet Clay (1978)
A Mother and Two Daughters (1982)
The Finishing School (1985)
A Southern Family (1987)
Father Melancholy's Daughter (1991)
The Good Husband (1994)
Evensong (1999)
Evenings at Five (2003)
Queen of the Underworld (2006)

Short-Story Collections

Dream Children (1976)
Mr. Bedford and the Muses (1983)

Nonfiction

Heart: A Personal Journey through Its Myths and Meanings (2001)
The Making of a Writer: The Journals of Gail Godwin (2007)

Research Sources

Encyclopedias and Handbooks: CA; CLC

"Gail Godwin," in *Dictionary of Literary Biography, Volume 6: American Novelists Since World War II, Second Series.* Detroit, MI: Gale, 1981. pp. 105–109.

"Gail Godwin," in *Dictionary of Literary Biography, Volume 234: American Short-Story Writers Since World War II, Third Series*. Detroit, MI: Gale, 2001. pp. 87–95.

Biographies and Interviews

Abbe, Elfrieda. "A Novelist and Her Journals." *The Writer.* May 2006. Available as a PDF from author's Web site. http://www.gailgodwin.com/pdfs/WRT-A0506.pdf. Last visited May 18, 2008.

"Featured Author: Gail Godwin." *New York Times.* http://www.nytimes.com/books/99/04/04/specials/godwin.html. Last visited May 18, 2008. Features an audio interview and links to book reviews.

Guidarini, Lisa. "An Interview with Author Gail Godwin." *Bluestalking Reader.* http://bluestalking.typepad.com/the_bluestalking_reader/2007/03/an_interview_wi_1.html. Last visited May 18, 2008.

Hale, Julie. "Heartfelt Look at a Symbol of Love." *BookPage.* Feb 2001. http://www.bookpage.com/0102bp/gail_godwin.html. Last visited May 18, 2008.

Wood, M. E. "Gail Godwin—Author Interview." *BellaOnline.* http://www.bellaonline.com/articles/art50333.asp. Last visited May 18, 2008.

Criticism and Readers' Guides

Cheney, Anne. "Gail Godwin and Her Novels." In *Southern Women Writers: The New Generation,* edited by Tonette Bond Inge. Tuscaloosa: University of Alabama Press, 1990, p. 204.

Emerick, Ron. "Theo and the road to sainthood in Gail Godwin's A Southern Family." *Southern Literary Journal* (33:2) 2001, 134–145.

Kissel, Susan S. *Moving On: The Heroines of Shirley Ann Grau, Anne Tyler, and Gail Godwin.* Bowling Green, OH: Bowling Green State University Popular Press, 1996.

Reader's guide for *The Finishing School. Random House.* http://www.randomhouse.com/catalog/display.pperl?isbn=9780345431905&view=rg. Last visited May 18, 2008.

Reader's guide for *The Odd Woman. Random House.* http://www.randomhouse.com/catalog/display.pperl?isbn=9780345389916&view=rg. Last visited May 18, 2008.

Reading group guide for *Evensong. Reading Group Guides.* http://www.readinggroupguides.com/guides_E/evensong1.asp. Last visited May 18, 2008.

Xie, Lihong. *The Evolving Self in the Novels of Gail Godwin.* Baton Rouge: Louisiana State University Press, 1995.

Web Sites

Gail Godwin Official Web Site. http://www.gailgodwin.com. Last visited May 18, 2008. Features extensive information about the author and her works.

Gail Godwin Video Webcast. *Library of Congress.* http://www.loc.gov/
    bookfest/2001/godwin.html. Last Visited June 20, 2008. Video clip of
    Godwin at the 2001 National Book Festival.

Olivia Goldsmith (1949–2004)
Glitz and Glamour
Biographical Sketch

Olivia Goldsmith was born Randy Goldfield in 1949 (some sources say 1954)
in Dumont, New Jersey (some sources say New York). She legally changed
her name to Justine Rendal, and used Olivia Goldsmith as her pen name.
After a painful divorce, she wrote her first novel, *First Wives Club,* which was
rejected by more than 20 publishers before being published to great success in
1992; and even being made into a movie in 1996. Goldsmith's novels feature
strong, sassy women, often with troubled pasts or secrets. She died unexpect-
edly from surgical complications, on January 15, 2004.

> It's all about aging and death and sexuality. What else is there, after
> all—except perhaps food? (Olivia Goldsmith, *Publishers Weekly* inter-
> view, 1996)

Major Works

Novels

The First Wives Club (1992)
Flavor of the Month (1993)
Fashionably Late (1994)
Simple Isn't Easy (1995)
The Bestseller (1996)
Marrying Mom (1996)
Switcheroo (1998)
Young Wives (2000)
Bad Boy (2001)
Pen Pals (2002)
Dumping Billy (2004)
Wish Upon a Star (2004)

Research Sources

Encyclopedias and Handbooks: CA

Biographies and Interviews

Baker, John F. "Olivia Goldsmith: The Road to Book-Tour Hell." *Publishers
    Weekly* (243:32) August 5, 1996, 417.

Fabrikant, Geraldine. "Once Burned, The First Wife Is Twice Shy." *New York Times*, October 27, 1996. Available online at http://query.nytimes.com/gst/fullpage.html?res=9A0DE0D81E30F934A15753C1A960958260. Last visited May 16, 2008.

Goldsmith, Olivia. "On Writing a Bestseller." *The Writer* (109:8) August 1996, 13.

"Olivia Goldsmith." *The Guardian (UK)*. http://www.guardian.co.uk/news/2004/jan/20/guardianobituaries.booksobituaries. Last visited May 16, 2008. Obituary.

Web Sites

Gardner, Ralph Jr. "Looks to Die For." *New York Magazine*. February 9, 2004. Available online at http://nymag.com/nymetro/news/features/n_9852/. Last visited June 27, 2008. A feature on her life and unexpected death.

Goldsmith, Olivia. "Bad Boyfriend Bootcamp." *Vaguepolitix*. http://www.vaguepolitix.com/crime/vision/vessay1.htm. Last visited January 20, 2008. Essay by Goldsmith.

Eileen Goudge (1950–)
Romantic Suspense
Biographical Sketch

Eileen Goudge was born on July 4, 1950, in San Mateo, California. A distant cousin of author Elizabeth Goudge, she was always interested in writing and began a career as a freelance journalist. After a stint on public aid as a single mother, Goudge became determined to become a fiction author. She began with teen romances, most famously titles in the *Sweet Valley High* series.

Her women's fiction features women dealing with relationships, often broken friendships or family secrets. Several of her novels have romantic suspense elements. Goudge lives in New York City.

> I find inspiration in my daily life. Look around you and you'll see a dozen different stories at any given time. The trick is to know which ones to write and to distill them into a story that others will be captivated by. (Eileen Goudge, *Bookreporter* interview. July 2007. http://www.bookreporter.com/authors/au-goudge-eileen.asp. Last visited June 30, 2008)

Major Works

Novels

Garden of Lies (1989)
Such Devoted Sisters (1992)

Blessing in Disguise (1994)
Trail of Secrets (1996)
Thorns of Truth (1998)
One Last Dance (1999)
The Second Silence (2000)
Carson Springs Trilogy: *Stranger in Paradise* (2001), *Taste of Honey* (2002),
    Wish Come True (2003)
Otherwise Engaged (2005)
Immediate Family (2006)
Woman in Red (2007)
Domestic Affairs (2008)

Research Sources

Encyclopedias and Handbooks: CA

Biographies and Interviews

Dhue, Laurie. "Goudge's Life Mirrors Amazing Fiction." *CNN.* April 27,
    1998. Available online at http://www.cnn.com/books/dialogue/9804/
    goudge/index.html. Last visited June 30, 2008.
"Eileen Goudge." *Barnes and Noble Studio.* http://media.barnesandnoble.com/?fr_
    story=797aee8ba5016ac21a273a6a7e4e4c1361c69c85&rf=sitemap.
    Last visited June 30, 2008. Video interview clip.
"Eileen Goudge." *Bookreporter.* http://www.bookreporter.com/authors/au-
    goudge-eileen.asp. Last visited June 30, 2008.
"An Interview with Eileen Goudge Discussing Domestic Affairs." *Perseus
    Books Group.* http://www.perseuspodcasts.com/main/podcasts/book.
    php?isbn=9781593154752. Last visited June 30, 2008. Audio interview clip.
Jaros, Tony. "Blessing in Disguise: Novelist Eileen Goudge's Years of Poverty
    Spurred Her To Success." *Vegetarian Times.* August 1995. Available on-
    line at http://findarticles.com/p/articles/mi_m0820/is_n216/ai_17326722.
    Last visited June 30, 2008.

Criticism and Readers' Guides

Reading group guide for *Woman in Red. Reading Group Guides.* http://www.
    readinggroupguides.com/guides3/woman_in_red1.asp. Last visited
    June 30, 2008.

Web Sites

Eileen Goudge Official Web Site. http://www.eileengoudge.com/. Last visited
    June 30, 2008. Features biography, book information, videos, and photo
    gallery.

Jane Green (1968–)
Chick Lit; Women's Romantic Fiction
Biographical Sketch

Jane Green was born on May 31, 1968, in London, England. She worked as a journalist in England before publishing her first book there, *Straight Talking,* in 1995. She continued to publish bestselling chick lit in the United Kingdom and her first American release came in 2000, *Jemima J: A Novel About Ugly Ducklings and Swans.*

Green's novels, usually set in Great Britain, feature young women dealing with friendships, jobs, family issues, and romantic relationships. She successfully blends witty dialogue and humorous situations with more serious issues, such as infidelity and loss. Her first three novels are decidedly chick lit, but the rest have a more mature feel to them and cover stronger issues. Green currently lives in Westport, Connecticut.

> The first person I sent my book to wrote back to say the characters were immature, the situations unrealistic, and the book was, "frankly unpublishable." Nine bestsellers later, I would say never let one person's opinion put you off or stop you from pursuing a passion. (Jane Green, *The Writers Life* interview, 2007. http://thewriterslife.blogspot.com/2007/07/author-interview-jane-green-author-of.html. Last visited May 18, 2008)

Major Works

Novels

Jemima J: A Novel about Ugly Ducklings and Swans (1999)
Mr. Maybe (1999)
Bookends (2002)
Babyville (2003)
Straight Talking (2003; first published in the United Kingdom in 1995)
To Have and To Hold (2004)
The Other Woman (2005)
Swapping Lives (2006)
Second Chance (2007)
The Beach House (2008)

Research Sources

Encyclopedias and Handbooks: CA

Biographies and Interviews

"Jane Green." *Barnes and Noble Meet the Writers.* http://www.barnesandnoble.com/writers/writer.asp?z=y&cid=716053. Last visited May 18, 2008.

Features extensive author information including interview and "Favorite Writers and Reads."

Thompson, Dorothy. "Author Interview—Jane Green." *The Writer's Life.* July 9, 2007. http://thewriterslife.blogspot.com/2007/07/author-interview-jane-green-author-of.html. Last visited May 18, 2008.

Criticism and Readers' Guides

Reading group guide for *The Other Woman. Reading Group Guides.* http://www.readinggroupguides.com/guides3/the_other_woman1.asp. Last visited May 18, 2008.

Reading guide for *Second Chance. Penguin.* http://us.penguingroup.com/static/rguides/us/second_chance.html. Last visited May 18, 2008.

Wells, Kim. "Fairy Tales for Feminists: Jane Green's *Jemima J* and Ugly Duckling to Swans." *WomenWriters.* http://www.womenwriters.net/bookreviews/wellsfairytale.html. Last visited May 18, 2008.

Web Sites

Jane Green" *Random House.* Publisher's Web site. http://www.randomhouse.com/features/janegreen/.

"Jane Green." *Trashionista.* http://www.trashionista.com/jane_green/index.html. Last visited May 18, 2008. Book blog featured page on Jane Green.

Jane Green Official Web Site. http://www.janegreen.com/. Last visited May 18, 2008. Features fan forum and author photo gallery.

If You Like Jane Green

Not to be dismissed simply as "fluff" chick lit, Green's novels, often set in Great Britain, feature young women dealing with friendships, jobs, family issues, and romantic relationships. While keeping a fun sense of humor, she also tackles more serious issues, such as infidelity, in her novel *To Have and To Hold,* and different facets of motherhood in *The Other Woman* and *Babyville.*

Then You Might Like

Barbara Delinsky. While not on the same humor level as Green, Delinsky's character-driven novels of everyday women dealing with events have the same storytelling style as Green, and Delinsky's earlier romances may also hold appeal for Green's fans.

Marian Keyes. Keyes displays much of the same sense of wit that Green does, and her novels share similar British and Irish settings that will appeal to Green's readers.

Sophie Kinsella. Kinsella's stand-alone novels, such as *Remember Me?,* the story of a woman who wakes up from an accident and can't remember the last three years of her life, will appeal to readers who enjoy Green's sense of humor. They are also set in Great Britain and feature likeable characters.

Jennifer Weiner. Weiner is known for giving her characters real personalities and quirks as well as for her sense of humor. Her intelligent chick lit is right on track with Green's more substantial take on the category.

Kristin Hannah (1960–)
Women's Romantic Fiction

Biographical Sketch

Kristin Hannah was born on September 25, 1960, in Garden Grove, California. She holds a J.D. from the University of Puget Sound, and completed her first novel (unpublished) while in law school. During her first pregnancy, while on bed rest from her law career, she turned to writing to keep from being bored. Hannah's novels are often considered romances (and her earlier paperback releases truly are); however, the family relationships and the issues that her characters must overcome are hallmarks of women's fiction. She writes about love and loss, complicated relationships, family secrets, and her novels are often tearjerkers.

She has won the Maggie Award and the RITA/Golden Heart Award from Romance Writers of America; a National Readers' Choice Award; and her novel *Home Again* was named *Publishers Weekly* Best Book of 1996, and *Booklist* Best Book of 1996. She lives on Bainbridge Island, Washington.

> I loved writing the romance novels, but I've always had a short attention span. . . . I wanted to write love stories—then and now—but I wanted some of those loves to be between mothers and daughters, fathers and sons, best friends, etc. More storylines, more characters, more issues. My books now tend to be about women coming of age, whenever that happens in their life. More often than not, they fall in love along the way, but that love is a peripheral part of the journey, not the journey itself. (Kristin Hannah, http://www.kristinhannah.com/content/faq. asp. Last visited May 18, 2008)

Major Works

Novels

On Mystic Lake (1999)
Angel Falls (2000)
Summer Island (2001)
Distant Shores (2002)
Between Sisters (2003)

The Things We Do for Love (2004)
Comfort and Joy (2005)
Magic Time (2006)
Firefly Lane (2008)

Research Sources

Encyclopedias and Handbooks: CA

Biographies and Interviews

"Author Answers with Kristin Hannah." *Word Nerd.* http://bkwriter.blog spot. com/2008/02/author-answers-with-kristin-hannah.html. Last visited May 18, 2008.

Holstine, Lesa. "Interview with Kristin Hannah." *Lesa's Book Critiques.* February 4, 2008. http://lesasbookcritiques.blogspot.com/2008/02/interview-with-kristin-hannah.html. Last visited May 18, 2008.

"Kristin Hannah." *Bookreporter.* http://www.bookreporter.com/authors/au-hannah-kristin.asp. Last visited May 18, 2008. Features bio and several author interviews.

Criticism and Readers' Guides

Reading group guide for *Firefly Lane. Reading Group Guides.* http://www.readinggroupguides.com/guides_F/firefly_lane1.asp. Last visited May 18, 2008.

Reading group guide for *The Things We Do For Love. Reading Group Guides.* http://www.readinggroupguides.com/guides3/things_we_do1.asp. Last visited May 18, 2008.

Web Sites

"Kristin Hannah." *Random House.* http://www.randomhouse.com/author/results.pperl?authorid=11819. Last visited May 18, 2008.

Kristin Hannah Official Web Site. http://www.kristinhannah.com/content/index.asp. Last visited May 18, 2008. Features author's blog, photo gallery, and information for book clubs.

Joanne Harris (1964–)

Mainstream

Biographical Sketch

Joanne Harris was born on March 7, 1964, in Barnsley, England. She worked briefly as an accountant and a teacher, and published her breakout novel,

Chocolat, in 1999,which was nominated for the Whitbread Prize. It was made into a movie in 2000.

Harris's novels feature magical realism, fantasy and mystery elements, and whimsical female characters. She currently lives in Huddersfield, England.

> I've always written. As a child and an adolescent I began by copying the writers I most admired, then I began slowly to find my own style. It took awhile, but eventually it began to emerge when I was in my twenties, although it wasn't until very recently that I felt confident enough to take the plunge and try to make a living from writing books. Until *Chocolat,* the thought had never crossed my mind; I liked my teaching job; I enjoyed writing in my spare time, and until then the two things had been perfectly compatible. (Joanne Harris, http://www.joanne-harris. co.uk/pages/faq.html. Last visited September 15, 2008)

Major Works

Novels

The Evil Seed (1992)
Sleep, Pale Sister (1994)
Chocolat (1999)
Blackberry Wine (2000)
Five Quarters of the Orange (2001)
Coastliners (2002)
Holy Fools (2004)
Gentlemen and Players (2006)
The Girl with No Shadow (2008)

Short-Story Collection

Jigs and Reels: Stories (2004)

Research Sources

Encyclopedias and Handbooks: CA

Biographies and Interviews

Antieau, Kim. "Interview with Joanne Harris." *Kim Antieau.* April 27, 2008. http://www.kimantieau.com/2008/04/interview-with-joanne-harris.html. Last visited September 19, 2008.

Gilson, Nancy. "Novelist Builds Upon Rich Flavor of *Chocolat.*" *Columbus Dispatch.* April 27, 2008. http://dispatch.com/live/content/arts/stories/2008/ 04/27/1_JOANNE_HARRIS.ART_ART_04–27–08_E1_17A0APR. html?sid=101. Last visited September 18, 2008.

Girish, Uma. "An Interview with Joanne Harris." *California Literary Review.* March 30, 2007. http://calitreview.com/56. Last visited September 15, 2008.

"Joanne Harris." *WritersFM.* http://www.writersfm.com/writersfm/podcasts. aspx. Last visited September 15, 2008. Podcast interview.

MacDonald, Jay. "Paris Match." *BookPage.* April 2008. http://www.book page. com/0804bp/joanne_harris.html. Last visited September 26, 2008.

Webster, Dan. "Interview with Joanne Harris." *Spokesman Review.* January 12, 2006. http://www.spokesmanreview.com/breaking/story.asp?id=5757. Last visited September 15, 2008.

Web Sites

"Joanne Harris." *Fora.tv.* http://fora.tv/2006/01/16/Joanne_Harris. Last visited September 18, 2008. 26-minute video clip of Harris at a book event.

"Joanne Harris." *MySpace.com.* http://www.myspace.com/keyserzozie. Last visited September 13, 2008. Author's official MySpace page, featuring blog and updates.

Joanne Harris Official Web Site. http://www.joanne-harris.co.uk/. Last visited September 15, 2008. Features FAQ, eight short stories, and photo gallery.

Jane Heller (1950–)
Humorous
Biographical Sketch

Jane Heller spent 10 years marketing other people's books before becoming a writer herself. Formerly a publicity executive for NAL, Dell, and Jove, she published her first book, *Cha Cha Cha* in 1993, and has published a novel per year since.

Heller's romantic comedies feature sharp dialogue, funny situations, and strong female characters. She lives in Santa Barbara, California.

The best thing that happened in my career was getting booked on the Today show when *Cha Cha Cha* came out. I was so psyched, because I'd spent a decade working at NY publishing houses promoting authors and getting THEM on the Today show. So now it was my turn. The worst thing that happened in my career was getting booked on the Today show for *Cha Cha Cha*! Turns out it's much easier to promote someone else's novel than sell your own on national TV. I was a nervous wreck! (Jane Heller, interview, http://conversationsfamouspeople. blogspot.com/2005/07/exclusive-interview-with-best-selling.html. Last visited May 19, 2008)

Major Works

Novels

Cha Cha Cha (1994)
The Club (1995)
Infernal Affairs (1996)
Princess Charming (1997)
Crystal Clear (1998)
Sis Boom Bah (1999)
Name Dropping (2000)
Female Intelligence (2001)
The Secret Ingredient (2002)
Lucky Stars (2003)
Best Enemies (2004)
An Ex to Grind (2005)
Some Nerve (2006)

Research Sources

Encyclopedias and Handbooks: CA

Biographies and Interviews

Bokma, Cindy. Interview. *Conversations about Famous People.* July 1, 2005. http://conversationsfamouspeople.blogspot.com/2005/07/exclusive-interview-with-best-selling.html. Last visited May 19, 2008.
"Jane Heller, Novelist/Volunteer." *Brightcove.* http://www.brightcove.tv/title.jsp?title=450195176&channel=307708985. Last visited May 19, 2008. Features a video segment on the author's experience volunteering while researching a character for a book.
"Jane Heller Speaks about *Female Intelligence.*" *BookBrowse.* http://www.bookbrowse.com/author_interviews/full/index.cfm?author_number=604. Last visited May 19, 2008.

Web Sites

"Jane Heller." *Authors On The Web.* http://www.Authorsontheweb.com/features/summer03/heller_jane.asp. Last visited May 19, 2008.
"Jane Heller." *HarperCollins.com.* http://www.harpercollins.com/authors/27553/Jane_Heller/index.aspx. Last visited May 19, 2008. Publisher's Web site.
The Official Jane Heller Web Site. http://www.janeheller.com/index2.htm. Last visited May 19, 2008. Features author information, bibliography, and e-mail contact form.

Lynne Hinton
Gentle

Biographical Sketch

Lynne Hinton was born in Dunham, North Carolina. An ordained minister, she has served as a hospice chaplain as well as the pastor of several congregations. While at seminary, she took literature classes and decided she wanted to be a writer as well.

Her novels are considered Christian fiction, and feature strong women and issues that relate to family and friendship. She lives in Albuquerque, New Mexico, and currently serves as the pastor of St. Paul's United Church of Christ.

> I believe it is vital for people of faith to know the stories of others. How can we speak of deeply spiritual issues like hope and peace if we are not willing to open our hearts and minds to the suffering and the triumphs of those who appear different from us? Stories serve to remind us that we are all a part of one human family. (Lynne Hinton, http://www. lynnehinton.com/about_lynne.html. Last visited May 19, 2008)

Major Works

Novels

The Things I Know Best (2001)
The Last Odd Day (2004)
The Arms of God (2005)
Hope Springs Trilogy: *Friendship Cake* (2000), *Hope Springs* (2002), *Forever Friends* (2003)
(As Jackie Lynn) Shady Grove Mysteries: *Down by the Riverside* (2006), *Jacob's Ladder: A Shady Grove Mystery* (2007), *Swing Low, Sweet Chariot* (2008)

Nonfiction

Meditations for Walking (1999)

Research Sources

Encyclopedias and Handbooks: CA

Biographies and Interviews

"Bestselling Novelist Lynne Hinton." *Godwin Memorial Library Blog.* http:// godwinlibrary.blog-city.com/hinton.htm. Last visited May 19, 2008.
Dixon, Joyce. "Recipe for Friendship: An Interview with Novelist Lynne Hinton." *Southern Scribe.* http://www.southernscribe.com/zine/culture/ Hinton_Lynne.htm. Last visited May 19, 2008.

"Lynne Hinton." *Bookreporter.* http://www.bookreporter.com/authors/au-hinton-lynne.asp. Last visited May 19, 2008. Brief biography.

Smith, Janet. "Janet Smith Interviews Lynne Hinton." *The Writer's E-Zine.* April, 2003. http://thewritersezine.com/t-zero/archives/2003-texts/2003-04-author.shtml. Last visited May 19, 2008.

Criticism and Readers' Guides

Reading group guide for *Friendship Cake. Reading Group Guides.* http://www.readinggroupguides.com/guides_F/friendship_cake1.asp. Last visited May 19, 2008.

Web Sites

Hinton, Lynne. "Writing as a Spiritual Discipline." *Critique Magazine.* http://www.critiquemagazine.com/onwriting/hinton.html. Last visited May 19, 2008.

"Lynne Hinton." *Authors On The Web.* http://www.kjexplorations.com/features/summer02/hinton.asp. Last visited May 19, 2008.

"Lynne Hinton." *HarperCollins.com.* http://www.harpercollins.com/authors/18409/Lynne_Hinton/index.aspx. Last visited May 19, 2008. Publisher Web site.

Lynne Hinton Official Web Site. http://www.lynnehinton.com/index.html. Last visited May 19, 2008.

Alice Hoffman (1952–)

Mainstream

Biographical Sketch

Alice Hoffman was born on March 16, 1952, in New York City. She has a B.A. in English and Anthropology from Adelphi University, and an M.A. in Creative Writing from Stanford University Creative Writing Center. Several of her novels, including *Practical Magic* and *Aquamarine,* have been made into movies.

Hoffman's novels are often filled with elements of magical realism; and her writing can be said to have fairy tale qualities. Usually considered a literary writer, her novels feature strong and intelligent female characters who find their mundane everyday lives disrupted by drama and/or magic. She lives in Boston and New York City.

The novel becomes the world that I live in. The creation of that other world—and the characters who live there—is very personal and very private. I don't discuss my work when I'm writing. I know too many people who have "talked out" a book, confused themselves with other people's perceptions during that delicate time when it's all too easy to throw a novel away. (Alice Hoffman. http://www.alicehoffman.com/blog/. Last visited May 19, 2008)

Major Works

Novels

Property Of (1977)
The Drowning Season (1979)
Angel Landing (1980)
White Horses (1982)
Fortune's Daughter (1985)
Illumination Night (1987)
At Risk (1988)
Seventh Heaven (1990)
Turtle Moon (1992)
Second Nature (1994)
Practical Magic (1995)
Here on Earth (1997)
Local Girls (1999)
The River King (2000)
Blue Diary (2001)
The Probable Future (2003)
Blackbird House (2004)
The Ice Queen (2005)
Skylight Confessions (2007)
The Third Angel (2008)

Research Sources

Encyclopedias and Handbooks: CA

"Alice Hoffman," in *Dictionary of Literary Biography, Volume 292: Twenty-First-Century American Novelists.* Detroit, MI: Gale, 2004. pp. 164–172.

Biographies and Interviews

"Alice Hoffman." *Barnes and Noble Meet the Writers.* http://www.barnesand noble.com/writers/writer.asp?cid=698183. Last visited May 19, 2008. Features audio interview and Hoffman's reading recommendations.
"Alice Hoffman." *BookBrowse.* http://www.bookbrowse.com/biographies/ index.cfm?author_number=366. Last visited May 19, 2008.
"Alice Hoffman." *Book Reporter.* http://www.bookreporter.com/authors/au-hoffman-alice.asp. Last visited May 19, 2008. Features 2 interviews.

Antieau, Kim. "Interview with Alice Hoffman." *Kim Antieau.* April 24, 2008. http://www.kimantieau.com/2008/04/interview-with-alice-hoffman. html. Last visited May 19, 2008.

"Featured Author: Alice Hoffman." *New York Times.* http://www.nytimes. com/books/99/06/13/specials/hoffman.html. Last visited May 19, 2008. Features links to several articles and reviews.

Lautman, Victoria. "Writers on the Record with Victoria Lautman." *Victoria Lautman Productions.* http://www.victorialautman.com/ontherecord. shtml#hoffman. Last visited May 19, 2008. Audio interview.

Reichl, Ruth. "At Home with Alice Hoffman: A Writer Set Free by Magic," *New York Times,* February 10, 1994, p. C1.

Wired for Books. "Alice Hoffman Interview with Don Swain 1988." http:// wiredforbooks.org/alicehoffman/. Last visited May 19, 2008. Audio interview.

Web Sites

Alice Hoffman Official Web Site. http://www.alicehoffman.com/. Last visited May 19, 2008. Features podcasts and author's blog.

Ann Hood (1956–)
Mainstream
Biographical Sketch

Ann Hood was born on December 9, 1956, in West Warwick, Rhode Island. She was a TWA flight attendant for 10 years before achieving her childhood ambition of becoming a writer. Her novels feature women handling family issues, enjoying friendships, and dealing with the complexities of life. She has won a Best American Spiritual Writing Award; a Paul Bowles Prize for Short Fiction; and two Pushcart Prizes. She has also written many articles for magazines such as *Redbook, Good Housekeeping, Ladies Home Journal, Ploughshares,* and *Paris Review.*

In 2002, Hood lost her five-year-old daughter, Grace, who died from a virulent form of strep. She turned to writing to ease her grief, penning a fictional account of a mother who loses her young daughter, *The Knitting Circle,* and a nonfiction work on the topic as well, *Comfort: A Journey Through Grief.* Hood lives in Providence, Rhode Island.

> Writing is like breathing to me; I don't have a choice—I just do it and love doing it. As a flight attendant, I carried a notebook with me and wrote on the subway out to the airport, on the plane, and in hotels on layovers. In fact, that's where I wrote *Somewhere Off the Coast of Maine.* (Ann Hood, *Contemporary Authors*)

Major Works

Novels

Somewhere off the Coast of Maine (1987)
Waiting to Vanish (1988)
Three-Legged Horse (1989)
Something Blue (1991)
Places to Stay the Night (1993)
The Properties of Water (1995)
Ruby (1998)
The Knitting Circle (2007)

Nonfiction

Do Not Go Gentle: My Search for Miracles in a Cynical Time (2000)
Comfort: A Journey Through Grief (2008)

Short-Story Collection

An Ornithologist's Guide to Life (2004)

Research Sources

Encyclopedias and Handbooks: CA

Biographies and Interviews

"Ann Hood: A Career in Midair." *Publishers Weekly.* October 12, 1998. Available online at http://www.publishersweekly.com/article/CA166132.html. Last visited May 19, 2008.

Reeser, Cynthia. "Spinning Grief into Threads: An Interview with Ann Hood on *The Knitting Circle*." *Prick of the Spindle.* October 2007. http://www.prickofthespindle.com/interviews/1.3/ann_hood_interview.htm. Last visited May 19, 2008.

Criticism and Readers' Guides

Reading group guide for *The Knitting Circle. W.W. Norton.* http://www2.wwnorton.com/rgguides/knittingcirclergg.htm. Last visited May 19, 2008.

Web Sites

Ann Hood Official Web Site. http://www.annhood.us/. Last visited May 19, 2008. Features biography, links, and author blog.

Hood, Ann. "I Married a Republican." *New York Times.* February 17, 2008. Available online at http://www.nytimes.com/2008/02/17/fashion/17love. html?_r=2&scp=1&sq=i+married+a+republican&st=nyt&oref=slo gin&oref=slogin. Last visited May 19, 2008.

Memmott, Carol. "Author's Grief Draws Circle." *USA Today.* January 22, 2007. Available online at http://www.usatoday.com/life/books/news/2007-01-22-knitting-circle_x.htm. Last visited May 19, 2008.

Rona Jaffe (1931–2005)

Mainstream

Biographical Sketch

Rona Jaffe was born on June 12, 1931, in Brooklyn, New York. Her first book, *The Best of Everything,* followed the lives of three young women finding their way in New York City in the late 1950s. It was made into a movie in 1959. Her novels, often set in New York City, focus mainly on conflicts in male–female relationships. She also wrote for *Cosmopolitan* in the 1960s.

In 1995 she established the Rona Jaffe Foundation Writer's Awards, providing grants to emerging women writers as they pursue their dreams of becoming authors. It is the only national literary awards program dedicated exclusively to supporting women writers. Jaffe died of cancer on December 30, 2005.

Major Works

Novels

The Best of Everything (1958)
Away from Home (1960)
The Cherry in the Martini (1966)
The Fame Game (1969)
The Other Woman (1972)
Family Secrets (1974)
The Last Chance (1976)
Class Reunion (1979)
Mazes and Monsters (1981)
After the Reunion (1985)
An American Love Story (1990)
The Cousins (1995)
Five Women (1997)
The Road Taken (2000)
The Room-Mating Season (2003)

Research Sources

Encyclopedias and Handbooks: CA

Biographies and Interviews

Owens, Mitchell. "Rona Jaffe, Author of Popular Novels, Is Dead at 74." *New York Times.* December 31, 2005. Available online at http://www. nytimes.com/2005/12/31/arts/31jaffe.html?ex=1293685200&en=ed58627 bd8c08097&ei=5090. Last visited September 27, 2008. Obituary.

"Rona Jaffe." *Harlequin.* http://www.eharlequin.com/author.html;jsessionid= 34477A146FCF0443DE1E10E4F6EA6CCF?authorid=784. Last visited March 9, 2009.

"Rona Jaffe." *Power Surge Live!.* http://www.power-surge.com/transcripts/ jaffe.htm. Last visited March 9, 2009.

Web Sites

Rona Jaffe Foundation. http://www.ronajaffefoundation.org/. Last visited September 28, 2008.

Rona Jaffe Official Web Site. http://ronajaffe.com/. Last visited September 28, 2008.

Cathy Kelly (1966–)

Mainstream

Biographical Sketch

Cathy Kelly was born on September 12, 1966, in Belfast, Ireland. She began her writing career as a reporter for Ireland's *Sunday World,* where she was named Young Journalist of the Year in 1986. She is still a columnist for the paper, headlining the "Dear Cathy" advice column. After publishing several bestselling novels in the United Kingdom, *Someone Like You* became her first U.S. release.

Kelly's novels feature a variety of female characters, of all ages and backgrounds, all dealing with families and friendship, all set in Ireland. In 2005, Kelly was appointed as a UNICEF Ireland Ambassador, and spends time traveling to Africa and promoting AIDS awareness. She currently lives in County Wicklow, Ireland.

> I've always been a voracious reader, and the sort of books I hated most were ones about these gilded, glamorous people who had loads of money, buckets of self-confidence and were stunningly beautiful. They never seemed real to me. So when I started to write, I wanted to write about people who were the opposite of that. My characters are normal people, with problems paying the mortgage and a huge load of ironing

waiting to be done. (Cathy Kelly, http://www.cathykelly.com/interviews. html. Last visited May 20, 2008)

Major Works

Novels

Woman to Woman (1997)
She's the One (1998)
Never Too Late (1999)
Someone like You (2000)
What She Wants (2003)
Best of Friends (2005)
Always and Forever (2005)
Just between Us (2006)

Research Sources

Encyclopedias and Handbooks: CA

Biographies and Interviews

Gadd, Denise. "From Agony Aunt to Novelist Mum." *The Age.* May 8, 2005. Available online at http://www.theage.com.au/news/Books/Novelist-mum/2005/05/05/1115092620983.html. Last visited May 20, 2008.

Wheatley, Jane. "A Superstar from Next Door." *The Times (London).* November 26, 2005. Available online at http://entertainment.timesonline.co.uk/tol/arts_and_entertainment/books/article596254.ecc. Last visited May 20, 2008.

Criticism and Readers' Guides

Reading guide for *Someone Like You. Penguin.* http://us.penguingroup.com/static/rguides/us/someone_like_you.html. Last visited May 20, 2008.

Web Sites

"Cathy Kelly." *Simon and Schuster.* http://www.simonsays.com/content/destination.cfm?tab=1&pid=365350. Last visited May 20, 2008. Publisher Web site.

Cathy Kelly Official Web Site. http://www.cathykelly.com/index.html. Last visited May 20, 2008. Features extensive author information including page of interviews and writing tips.

"Cathy Kelly's Diary from Mozambique." *Unicef.* http://www.unicef.ie/cathy-kelly-mozambique.htm. Last visited May 20, 2008.

"Cathy Kelly Visits Rwanda with Unicef Ireland." *Unicef.* http://www.unicef.ie/cathy_kelly_rwanda_1.htm. Last visited May 20, 2008.

Marian Keyes (1963–)
Chick Lit

Biographical Sketch

Marian Keyes was born on September 10, 1963, in Limerick, Ireland. She earned a law degree from University College Dublin, but never practiced, instead worked as a waitress and an accountant, writing short stories in her spare time and finally publishing her first novel, *Watermelon,* in the United Kingdom in 1995. Three years later (in 1998) the book was published in the United States to great acclaim, ushering in the wave of British chick lit along with Helen Fielding and others. Keyes's novels are very humorous, and feature everyday young Irish women navigating work issues, family problems, and relationships. Several of her novels (*Watermelon, Rachel's Holiday, Angels, Anybody Out There?*), while not a series, revolve around the sisters from the loving and funny Walsh family. She has also written three collections, combinations of short stories, essays, and columns; as well as contributing short stories to many chick lit anthologies.

Open about the fact that she had spent time in rehabilitation for alcohol abuse, Keyes has incorporated the issue into several of her novels. She currently lives in Dublin, Ireland.

> I was so lonely for so long and the alcoholism was so incredibly ugly and pointless and bleak, and oh, shabby, shabby! And it was so painful to live through, and I was so confused, I kept waiting to get into a clearing, and I never did—until I did. And then when I started to write, I had this incredible database of pain. I took that pain, and wrote about it—and people identified with it. Writing about feeling disconnected has enabled me to connect, and that has been the most lovely thing of all. (Marian Keyes, *Telegraph* interview. http://www.telegraph.co.uk/arts/main. jhtml?xml=/arts/2007/03/17/bokeyes117.xml. Last visited May 20, 2008)

Major Works

Novels

Watermelon (1995)
Lucy Sullivan is Getting Married (1996)
Rachel's Holiday (1998)
Last Chance Saloon (1999)
Sushi for Beginners (2000)
No Dress Rehearsal (2000)
Angels (2002)
The Other Side of the Story (2004)
Anybody Out There? (2006)
This Charming Man (2008)

Essay Collections

Under the Duvet (2001)
Further Under the Duvet (2005)
Cracks In My Foundation (2005)

Research Sources

Encyclopedias and Handbooks: CA

Biographies and Interviews

"Bestselling Irish Author's New Book." *BBC Radio 4.* Audio interview, BBC radio broadcast, May 1, 2008. http://www.bbc.co.uk/radio4/womanshour/03/2008_17_mon.shtml. Last visited May 20, 2008.

MacDonald, Marianne. "I Had this Incredible Database of Pain." *The Telegraph (UK).* March 17, 2007. Available online at http://www.telegraph.co.uk/arts/main.jhtml?xml=/arts/2007/03/17/bokeyes117.xml. Last visited May 20, 2008.

"Marian Keyes." *Bookreporter.* http://www.bookreporter.com/authors/au-keyes-marian.asp. Features brief biography and interview. Last visited November 18, 2008.

Nikkhah, Roya. "Marian Keyes Ready to Tackle Domestic Violence." *The Telegraph (UK).* April 20, 2008. Available online at http://www.telegraph.co.uk/arts/main.jhtml?xml=/arts/2008/04/20/bokeyes120.xml. Last visited May 20, 2008.

Scanlon, Anne Marie. "Marian Has the Keyes to the Secrets of Story-Telling." *The Independent (Ireland).* May 11, 2008. Available online at http://www.independent.ie/entertainment/books/marian-has-the-keyes-to-the-secrets-of-storytelling-1372308.html. Last visited May 20, 2008.

Web Sites

Marian Keyes Books. http://www.mariankeyesbooks.com/. Last visited May 20, 2008. Publisher Web site from HarperCollins. Features an unpublished short story, "The Seven Deadlies."

Marian Keyes Official Web Site. http://www.mariankeyes.com/. Last visited May 20, 2008. Features newsletter, Fact File, and links to recent interviews.

Cassandra King (1944–)

Mainstream

Biographical Sketch

Cassandra King was born on September 18, 1944, in Dothan, Alabama. She has worked as a college writing instructor and a human-interest reporter for a weekly paper in Alabama. Her novels feature strong Southern women and fun, often eccentric, characters in stories about friendships and family relationships.

King is married to writer Pat Conroy, and they live in South Carolina.

All my life I was a closet writer. It's all I wanted to do—and all I did, whenever I could slip off from my life and do so, but I lacked both confidence and courage, two necessity ingredients for success. I'm ashamed to say that I wouldn't stand up for myself, allow myself time to write or seek publication. It was only when I was in my 40s, went to graduate school, and was encouraged to share my work that I gained any kind of confidence. My master's thesis became my first novel, and I've been going full guns ever since. (Cassandra King, interview. http://www.barnesand noble.com/writers/writerdetails.asp?cid=909681#goodtoknow. Last visited May 22, 2008)

Major Works

Novels

The Sunday Wife (2002)
Making Waves (2004)
The Same Sweet Girls (2005)
Queen of Broken Hearts (2007)

Research Sources

Encyclopedias and Handbooks: CA

Biographies and Interviews

"Cassandra King." *Barnes and Noble Meet the Writers.* http://www.barne sandnoble.com/writers/writer.asp?cid=909681. Last visited May 22, 2008. Features interviews, book links, and trivia.
"Cassandra King." *Book Reporter.* http://www.bookreporter.com/authors/ au-king-cassandra.asp. Last visited May 22, 2008. Features brief biography and two interviews.
"Pat Conroy Interviews His Wife, Cassandra King." *Book Chase.* http:// bookchase.blogspot.com/2008/04/pat-conroy-interviews-his-wife.html. Last visited May 22, 2008. Video interview.
Zacharias, Karen Spears. "Cassandra King Speaks with Karen Spears Zacharias." *Authors Round the South.* December 26, 2006. http://www. authorsroundthesouth.com/index.php/author-2-author/38-author-news-a-interviews/138-cassandra-king-speaks-with-karen-spears-zacha rias. Last visited May 22, 2008.

Criticism and Readers' Guides

Reading group guide for *The Same Sweet Girls*. *Reading Group Guides*. http://www.readinggroupguides.com/guides3/same_sweet_girls1.asp. Last visited May 22, 2008.
Reading group guide for *The Sunday Wife*. *Reading Group Guides*. http://www.readinggroupguides.com/guides3/sunday_wife1.asp. Last visited May 22, 2008.

Web Sites

"Cassandra King." *Alabama Literary Map*. http://www.alabamaliterarymap.org/author.cfm?AuthorID=140. Last visited May 22, 2008. Brief biographical information, Web links.
Cassandra King Official Web Site. http://www.cassandrakingconroy.com/. Last visited May 22, 2008. Features photo album and guestbook.
Cassandra King Video Webcast. *Library of Congress*. http://www.loc.gov/bookfest/2003/king.html. Last visited May 22, 2008. Video clip of King at the 2003 National Book Festival.

Sophie Kinsella (1969–)
Chick Lit; Humorous
Biographical Sketch

Sophie Kinsella is the pen name of British author Madeline Wickham. She was born December 12, 1969, in London, England. She worked as a financial journalist before publishing fiction.

Under the name Kinsella, she writes the frothy and funny Shopaholic series, as well as several stand-alone breezy chick lit novels. Kinsella's chick lit is fast paced and features humorous dialogue and over-the-top situations, with young female characters. Using her birth name (Wickham), she writes women's fiction that is a bit more mature, featuring more serious topics and more mature characters. Her books are all set in England. She lives in Hertfordshire, England.

> I never really felt financial journalism was my true love, partly because I'm just not interested in the subject and partly because I've never been very good at sticking to facts. But I did love to write. I used to read novels avidly on the train—and one day I just decided to try and write one. As soon as I started, I knew I'd found the thing I wanted to do. (Sophie Kinsella, interview. http://www.teenreads.com/authors/au-kinsella-sophie.asp. Last visited May 22, 2008)

Major Works

Novels

Shopaholic Series: *Confessions of a Shopaholic* (2001), *Shopaholic Takes Manhattan* (2002), *Shopaholic Ties the Knot* (2003), *Shopaholic and Sister* (2005), *Shopaholic and Baby* (2007)
Can You Keep a Secret? (2004)
The Undomestic Goddess (2005)
Remember Me? (2008)

As Madeline Wickham

The Tennis Party (1995)
A Desirable Residence (1996)
Swimming Pool Sunday (1997)
The Gatecrasher (1998)
The Wedding Girl (1999)
Cocktails for Three (2000)
Sleeping Arrangements (2001)

Research Sources

Biographies and Interviews

Sachs, Andrea. "Between the Lines with Sophie Kinsella." *Time.* July 21, 2005. Available on line at http://www.time.com/time/columnist/sachs/article/0,9565,1085542,00.html. Last visited May 22, 2008.
"Sophie Kinsella." *Barnes and Noble Meet the Writers.* http://www.barnesand noble.com/writers/writer.asp?cid=1020738. Last visited May 22, 2008.
"Sophie Kinsella." *Book Reporter.* http://www.bookreporter.com/authors/au-kinsella-sophie.asp. Last visited May 22, 2008. Features two interviews.
"Sophie Kinsella Interview." *Teen Reads.* http://www.teenreads.com/authors/au-kinsella-sophie.asp. Last visited May 22, 2008.

Criticism and Readers' Guides

Scanlon, Jennifer. "Making Shopping Safe for the Rest of Us: Sophie Kinsella's Shopaholic Series and Its Readers." *Americana: The Journal of American Popular Culture 1900 to Present.* Fall 2005. Available online at http://www.americanpopularculture.com/journal/articles/fall_2005/scanlon.htm. Last visited May 22, 2008.

Web Sites

Sophie Forum. http://sophieforum.modwest.com/. Last visited May 22, 2008. Discussion forum for fans.

Sophie Kinsella Official Site. http://www.randomhouse.com/bantamdell/kin
    sella/. Last visited May 22, 2008. Features "Meet Sophie" forum, and
    multimedia links.
"Sophie Kinsella: The Book Show Episode 14." *The Book Show.* Available
    at http://www.youtube.com/watch?v=J9eg0JcOv0c. Last visited May 22,
    2008. Video clips of Kinsella.

Judith Krantz (1928–)
Glitz and Glamour
Biographical Sketch

Judith Krantz was born on January 9, 1928, in New York City. She received
a B.A. from Wellesley College, and from the 1940s through the 1970s, worked
as a publicist in Paris; an editor at *Good Housekeeping;* and as a contributing
writer to *McCall's, Ladies Home Journal*, and *Cosmopolitan*. At the age
of 51, she published her first novel, *Scruples,* which became an instant best
seller. The paperback reprint rights to her second novel, *Princess Daisy,* were
purchased by Bantam Books for over $3 million, setting a record for the high-
est price paid for the rights to a work of fiction.

Krantz's novels are known for their glitz and glamour, featuring beautiful,
rich, and powerful women, sexy love scenes, and soap opera drama levels.
Several of her novels were made into television mini-series in the 1980s,
including *Scruples* and *Princess Daisy.* Krantz lives in Beverly Hills.

> I get quite a lot of people who say, "oh, I don't read your kind of books,
> but I read you." I don't know what they think my kind of book is. One
> interviewer kept after me to say my books were in the same genre as
> Jackie Collins and Danielle Steel and Sidney Sheldon, and finally I said,
> "Look, this is going to sound very immodest, but I think my books are
> in a genre of their own. They're just my kind of book." After the inter-
> view was over, I realized I should have said that it's the genre of yummy,
> but I didn't think fast enough. (Judith Krantz, *Booklist* interview, 1992)

Major Works

Novels

Scruples (1978)
Princess Daisy (1980)
Mistral's Daughter (1982)
I'll Take Manhattan (1986)
Till We Meet Again (1988)
Dazzle (1990)
Scruples Two (1992)

Lovers (1994)
Spring Collection (1996)
The Jewels of Tessa Kent (1998)

Other Works of Interest

Sex and Shopping: Confessions of a Nice Jewish Girl. New York: St. Martin's. 2000.

Research Sources

Encyclopedias and Handbooks: CA

Biographies and Interviews

"The Booklist Interview: Judith Krantz." *Booklist* (89:3) October 1, 1992, 240–241.

Higgins, Bill. "Success Stories: Wealth, Power, Beauty, Brains—Judith Krantz's Heroines Have It All," *Town & Country* (152:5222) 1998, 184–188.

Huseby, Sandy. "Judith Krantz: Life is Even Better than Fiction." *BookPage.* May 2000. http://www.BookPage.com/0005bp/judith_krantz.html. Last visited May 26, 2008.

Rosati, Arianna Pavia. "Sex and Glamour a la Judith Krantz." *New York Times.* April 7, 1996. Available online at http://query.nytimes.com/gst/fullpage.html?res=9D00E4D71339F934A35757C0A960958260. Last visited May 26, 2008.

Web Sites

"Judith Krantz." *Random House.* http://www.randomhouse.com/author/results.pperl?authorid=16236. Last visited May 26, 2008. Publisher Web site.

"Person of the Week: Judith Krantz." *Wellesley College.* http://www.welles ley.edu/Anniversary/krantz.html. Last visited May 26, 2008.

Lorna Landvik (1954–)

Family Stories; Humorous

Biographical Sketch

Lorna Landvik was born on December 12, 1954, in Grand Forks, North Dakota. Her family moved to Minnesota when she was three, and she sets many of her novels in that state. After moving to California, she performed stand-up comedy and briefly worked at the Playboy Mansion before returning to Minnesota and becoming a writer.

Landvik's novels feature eccentric characters, folksy stories, and charming homespun humor. She often features quirky families and strong communities—and her novels always have one character of Norwegian descent. Landvik currently lives in Minneapolis.

I think I've cried at some point in all of my books, which can be embar-
rassing if I'm writing in a public place. (Lorna Landvik, *Bookreporter*
interview, http://www.bookreporter.com/authors/au-landvik-lorna.asp.
Last Accessed May 28, 2008)

Major Works

Novels

Patty Jane's House of Curl (1995)
Your Oasis on Flame Lake (1997)
Tall Pine Polka (1999)
Welcome to the Great Mysterious (2000)
Angry Housewives Eating Bon Bons (2003)
Oh My Stars (2005)
The View from Mount Joy (2007)
'Tis The Season (2008)

Research Sources

Encyclopedias and Handbooks: CA

"Lorna Landvik," in *Dictionary of Literary Biography, Volume 292:
Twenty-First-Century American Novelists.* Detroit, MI: Gale, 2004.
pp. 215–221.

Biographies and Interviews

Baenen, Jeff. "Talking With: Lorna Landvik." *Milwaukee Journal Sentinel.*
December 29, 2007. Available online at http://www.jsonline.com/story/
index.aspx?id=701082. Last visited May 28, 2008.
Cary, Alice. "Good Gravy, Lorna Landvik is a Hoot!" *BookPage.* July 1997.
http://www.BookPage.com/9707bp/firstperson2.html. Last visited May
28, 2008.
Cornell, Tricia. "From the Beauty Parlor to the Barricades." *Minneapolis/St
Paul City Pages.* June 15, 2005. Available online at http://citypages.com/
databank/26/1280/article13407.asp. Last visited May 28, 2008.
"Lorna Landvik." *Bookreporter.* http://www.bookreporter.com/authors/au-
landvik-lorna.asp. Last visited May 28, 2008. Features interview and
"Behind the Writing."

Criticism and Readers' Guides

Reader's guide to *Your Oasis on Flame Lake. Random House.* http://www.
randomhouse.com/catalog/display.pperl?isbn=9780449002988&view=rg.
Last visited May 28, 2008.

Reading group guide to *Angry Housewives Eating Bon Bons. Reading Group Guides.* http://www.readinggroupguides.com/guides3/angry_housewives_eating1.asp. Last visited May 28, 2008.

Reading group guide to *Welcome to the Great Mysterious. Reading Group Guides.* http://www.readinggroupguides.com/guides3/welcome_great_mysterious1.asp. Last visited May 28, 2008.

Web Sites

"Lorna Landvik." *Random House.* http://www.randomhouse.com/features/lornalandvik/index.html. Last visited May 28, 2008. Author's official Web site, featuring newsletter, "Behind the Writing," and a section for book groups.

Billie Letts (1938–)
Mainstream
Biographical Sketch

Billie Letts was born on May 30, 1938, in Tulsa, Oklahoma. She received a B.A. from Southeast Missouri State College and an M.A. from Southeastern Oklahoma State University. Before publishing her first novel, she held various jobs, including working as a window washer, dance instructor, roller-skating car hop, secretary to a private detective, and teacher. *Where the Heart Is,* her first novel, was an Oprah's Book Club selection, a *New York Times* bestseller, and was made into a movie in 2000.

Letts's novels feature women overcoming adversity and finding family in the least likely places. She writes about average or poor American families, no glitz and glamour here. Her writing features a gentle sense of humor and always showcases eccentric casts of characters. *Where the Heart Is* won the Walker Percy Award from the New Orleans Writers Conference, as well as an Oklahoma Book Award. Letts lives in Durant, Oklahoma.

> I suppose I'd categorize my books as "slice of life" novels, what happens to my characters seems to me to be the result of living in the chaos of the real world. (Billie Letts, *Readers Read* Interview, http://www.readersread.com/features/billieletts2.htm. Last visited May 26, 2008)

Major Works

Novels

Where the Heart Is (1995)
The Honk and Holler Opening Soon (1998)
Shoot the Moon (2004)
Made In the USA (2008)

Other Works of Interest

"On Billie Letts." *Know Southern History.* http://www.knowsouthernhistory.
net/Culture/Literature/billie_letts.htm. Last visited May 26, 2008. Brief
personal essay by Letts.

"The Call That Changed My Life." *Readers Read.* http://www.readersread.
com/features/billieletts.htm. Last visited May 26, 2008. Brief essay detail-
ing how Letts felt when learning her first novel was an Oprah's Book
Club selection.

Research Sources

Encyclopedias and Handbooks: CA

Biographies and Interviews

"Interview with Billie Letts." *Readers Read.* http://www.readersread.com/fea
tures/billieletts2.htm. July 2004. Last visited May 26, 2008.

Witter, Dottie. "The 2004 Speaker Series featuring Billie Letts." *Oklahoma
State University.* http://www.library.okstate.edu/friends/cobb/letts.htm.
Last visited May 26, 2008.

Criticism and Readers' Guides

Reading group guide for *The Honk and Holler Opening Soon. Reading
Group Guides.* http://www.readinggroupguides.com/guides_H/honk_
and_holler1.asp. Last visited May 26, 2008.

Reading group guide for *Shoot the Moon. Reading Group Guides.* http://www.
readinggroupguides.com/guides3/shoot_the_moon1.asp. Last visited
May 26, 2008.

"*Where the Heart Is* by Billie Letts." *Oprah's Book Club.* http://www.oprah.com/
article/oprahsbookclub/pastselections/obc_19981207_review Last visited Nov
26, 2008. Features trivia links, online discussion, and discussion questions.

Web Sites

"Billie Letts." *Hachette Book Group.* http://www.hachettebookgroupusa.com/
authors_Billie-Letts-(1012944).htm. Last visited May 26, 2008. Publisher
Web site featuring brief biography and links to interviews.

Elinor Lipman (1950–)

Mainstream

Biographical Sketch

Elinor Lipman was born on October 16, 1950, in Lowell, Massachusetts. She
graduated from Simmons College and held several journalistic jobs, as well

as working as a writing instructor for several years before publishing fiction. Lipman's novels feature realistic, everyday women, and humor. They often deal with family and social issues. Her novels accurately reflect their times, acting as social satire.

In 2001 Lipman won the New England Book Award for fiction. She also received an Honorary Doctor of Letters from Simmons College in 2000. She lives in Manhattan and Northampton, Massachusetts.

> I take great pains with the writing. I rewrite every sentence one hundred times. I keep chipping away at it. I'm always looking to avoid what Henry James called "weak specifications." (Elinor Lipman, *Publishers Weekly* interview)

Major Works

Novels

Then She Found Me (1990)
The Way Men Act (1992)
Isabel's Bed (1995)
The Inn at Lake Devine (1998)
The Ladies' Man (1999)
The Dearly Departed (2001)
The Pursuit of Alice Thrift (2003)
My Latest Grievance (2006)

Short-Story Collection

Into Love and Out Again (1997)

Other Works of Interest

"My Book the Movie, or, I Seem to Be In a Tiny Minority of Authors Who Love Their Adaptation." *Huffington Post.* April 24, 2008. http://www. huffingtonpost.com/elinor-lipman/post_145_b_98502.html. Last visited June 1, 2008.

Research Sources

Encyclopedias and Handbooks: CA

Biographies and Interviews

Bargreen, Melinda. "Teenage Memories Serve Author Elinor Lipman Well." *Seattle Times.* June 7, 2006. Available online at http://community.seattle times.nwsource.com/archive/?date=20060607&slug=lipman07. Last visited June 1, 2008.

"Elinor Lipman." *Barnes and Noble Meet the Writers.* http://www.barnesand noble.com/writers/writer.asp?cid=1267662. Last visited June 1, 2008. Features interview and Lipman's reading recommendations.

"Ink: Q & A Elinor Lipman." *Powells.* http://www.powells.com/ink/lipman. html. Last visited June 1, 2008.

Scribner, Amy. "Elinor Lipman Proves Laughter is the Best Medicine." *Book-Page.* July 2003. http://www.BookPage.com/0307bp/elinor_lipman.html. Last visited June 1, 2008.

Steinberg, Sybil. "Love, Intricate and Off-Kilter: Elinor Lipman." *Publishers Weekly* (250:23) June 9, 2003, 31. Available online at http://www.publish ersweekly.com/article/CA303781.html. Last visited June 28, 2008.

Criticism and Readers' Guides

Reader's guide to *The Dearly Departed. Random House.* http://www.ran domhouse.com/catalog/display.pperl?isbn=9780375724589&view=rg. Last visited June 1, 2008.

Reading group guide for *The Inn at Lake Devine. Reading Group Guides.* http://www.readinggroupguides.com/guides_I/inn_at_lake_devine1.asp. Last visited June 1, 2008.

Reading group guide for *The Pursuit of Alice Thrift. Reading Group Guides.* http://www.readinggroupguides.com/guides3/pursuit_of_alice_thrift1. asp. Last visited June 1, 2008.

Web Sites

Kantrowitz, Anita K. "How Hollywood's Hunt 'Found' Elinor Lipman's Novel." *The Jewish Journal.* April 24, 2008. Available online at http:// www.jewishjournal.com/books/article/how_hollywoods_hunt_found_ elinor_lipmans_novel_20080425/. Last visited June 1, 2008.

A Suitable Web Site. http://www.elinorlipman.com/. Last visited June 1, 2008. Author's official Web site, featuring biography and essays.

If You Like Elinor Lipman

Lipman's novels featuring realistic women and humor deal with family and social issues. Her novels accurately reflect their times, acting as social satire. *The Inn at Lake Devine,* for example, tells the story of a young Jewish woman whose family is discouraged from summering at a Gentile resort, sparking in her a lifelong determination to break the rules.

Then You Might Like

Claire Cook. Cook's novels give readers humor, eccentric families, and everyday characters. Her novel *Life's a Beach* is the story of a woman who can't seem to get her act together—at 40, she's unemployed and still living in an apartment above her parents' garage.

Patricia Gaffney. Gaffney's novels feature smart and mature women and revolve around their friendships and family relationships. Clever dialogue and realistically drawn characters and situations engage readers. *Mad Dash,* the story of a marriage that may or may not be over, is a good match for Lipman's fans of social satire.

Jane Heller. Heller's sense of humor is sharper than Lipman's, but she writes realistic characters and her romantic comedies feature sharp dialogue, funny situations, and strong female characters.

Lorna Landvik. Landvik has the same sense of humor as Lipman and writes about families and communities dealing with the world around them. *Your Oasis on Flame Lake,* the story of characters living in a small Minnesota town, would appeal to those who like Lipman's storytelling and wry take on communities.

Mameve Medwed. A friend of Lipman's, Medwed writes in a very similar style. Her novels are contemporary and humorous, and feature everyday women dealing with family relationships. Considered modern comedies of manners, they are also very character driven.

Jill McCorkle (1958–)

Mainstream

Biographical Sketch

Jill McCorkle was born on July 7, 1958, in Lumberton, North Carolina. She worked as a teacher and a librarian in Florida and taught creative writing before publishing fiction. Most recently, she has worked as a professor of creative writing at Harvard University and Bennington College. Her fiction features strong Southern women, and showcases relationships, from friendships to the way people relate to the world around them. Her short stories have also been widely published in journals and magazines, and appear in many anthologies, along with her essays.

McCorkle has won the Jesse Rehder Prize from the University of North Carolina; the Andrew James Purdy Prize from Hollins College; the Jon Dos Passos Prize for Excellence in Literature; she has had five *New York Times* Notable Book of the Year citations; received the New England Booksellers' Association award for body of work; and North Carolina Award for Literature in 1999. She lives in Boston.

> I used to have a schedule—pre family—I got up and wrote from 5 to 8 every day then went to work. I realized when my daughter was born,

that I would not be able to keep that schedule but instead needed to be flexible. So I write when I can. I try to clear out nice big blocks of time during the school day or when I can steal away for a day or two, but most of the time I am engaging in what you call a more impressionistic manner. I take lots and lots of notes. I save and store until I get a big block of time and/or it feels like the top of my head will fly off—whichever comes first! (Jill McCorkle, *Southern Scribe* interview. http://www.southernscribe.com/zine/authors/McCorkle_Jill.htm. Last visited June 1, 2008)

Major Works

Novels

The Cheer Leader (1984)
July 7th (1984)
Tending to Virginia (1987)
Ferris Beach (1990)
Carolina Moon (1996)

Short-Story Collections

Crash Diet (1992)
Final Vinyl Days and Other Stories (1998)
Creatures of Habit (2001)

Other Works of Interest

"Cuss Time." *The American Scholar.* http://www.theamericanscholar.org/cuss-time/. Last visited March 11, 2009. Brief essay by McCorkle.

Research Sources

Encyclopedias and Handbooks: CA

"Jill McCorkle," in *Dictionary of Literary Biography, Volume 234: American Short-Story Writers Since World War II, Third Series.* Detroit, MI: Gale, 2001. pp. 186–196.

Biographies and Interviews

"Audio Interview with Jill McCorkle with Don Swaim, 1990." *Wired for Books.* http://wiredforbooks.org/jillmccorkle/index.htm. Last visited June 1, 2008. Audio interview clip.
"Jill McCorkle." *Know Southern History.* http://www.knowsouthernhistory. net/Culture/Literature/jill_mccorkle.htm. Last visited June 1, 2008.

Kingsbury, Pam. "Creature of the Writing Habit." *Southern Scribe.* http://www.southernscribe.com/zine/authors/McCorkle_Jill.htm. Last visited June 1, 2008.

McDaniel, Jill. "Jill McCorkle, Humanist Author." *Writers Write.* http://www.writerswrite.com/journal/jun00/mccorkle.htm. Last visited June 1, 2008.

"Today's Topic: Moments that Shape Our Lives with Jill McCorkle." *Washington Post Online.* July 30, 2000. http://www.washingtonpost.com/wp-srv/liveonline/00/magazine/mccorkle0731.htm. Last visited June 1, 2008. Transcript of live online chat with McCorkle.

Criticism and Readers' Guides

Bennett, Barbara. *Understanding Jill McCorkle.* Columbia: University of South Carolina Press. 2000.

Reading group guide for *Carolina Moon. Reading Group Guides.* http://readinggroupguides.com/guides_C/carolina_moon1.asp. Last visited June 1, 2008.

Reading group guide for *Final Vinyl Days. Reading Group Guides.* http://www.readinggroupguides.com/guides_F/final_vinyl_days1.asp. Last visited June 1, 2008.

Diane McKinney-Whetstone (1954–)
African American; Mainstream
Biographical Sketch

Diane McKinney-Whetstone was born in 1954 in Philadelphia. She graduated with a B.A. in English from the University of Pennsylvania and worked a as public affairs officer for the USDA Forest Service for several years before deciding to write fiction in her 40s. Her novels feature strong African American women and generations of close-knit families. They are set in Philadelphia in the middle of the 20th century.

McKinney-Whetstone won the Black Caucus of the American Library Association Literary Award for Fiction in 2005 and the Zora Neale Hurston Society Award for Creative Contribution to Literature in1997. She currently teaches fiction at the University of Pennsylvania and lives in Philadelphia.

I was approaching a significant birthday, and doing the life examination one does as the age of forty comes around. At the time, my professional writing involved public affairs and public relations, as well as "translating" scientific reports into lay terms audiences could understand. I realized this wasn't the type of writing I was burning to do, and if I didn't do it then,

I never would. I had written poetry in school, but creative writing was one of those things I always told myself I really wanted to do. Because I read a lot, it inspired me to want to do the same type of writing. (Diane McKinney-Whetstone, *Writers Write* interview, http://www.writerswrite. com/journal/oct00/whetstone.htm. Last visited June 1, 2008)

Major Works

Novels

Tumbling (1994)
Tempest Rising (1996)
Blues Dancing (1999)
Leaving Cecil Street (2001)
Trading Dreams at Midnight (2008)

Research Sources

Biographies and Interviews

"A Conversation with Diane McKinney-Whetstone." *Charlie Rose.* May 27, 1996. http://www.charlierose.com/shows/1996/05/27/4/a-conversation-with-diane-mckinney-whetstone. Last visited June 1, 2008. Video interview clip.

Dellasega, Cheryl. "Mothers Who Write: Diane McKinney-Whetstone." *Writers Write.* October/November 2000. http://www.writerswrite.com/journal/oct00/whetstone.htm. Last visited June 1, 2008.

"Diane McKinney-Whetstone." *Bill Thompson's Eye on Books.* http://www. eyeonbooks.com/ibp.php?ISBN=0688163858. Last visited June 1, 2008. Audio interview clip.

"Diane McKinney-Whetstone." *New Jersey Public Television and Radio.* June, 2004. http://www.njn.net/television/njnseries/anotherview/bookshelf/dianemckinney-whetstone.html. Last visited June 1, 2008. Video interview clip.

Lesinski, Jeanne M. "Diane McKinney-Whetstone." *Answers.com.* http://www. answers.com/topic/diane-mckinney-whetstone. Last visited June 1, 2008.

Criticism and Readers' Guides

"Another Philadelphia Story (South Philly, That Is)." *Penn Arts and Sciences.* Fall 1996. Available online at http://www.sas.upenn.edu/sasalum/news ltr/fall96/Philly.html. Last visited June 1, 2008.

"Diane McKinney-Whetstone." *Africana Research Center.* http://php.scripts. psu.edu/dept/arc//index.php?option=com_content&task=view&id=79& Itemid=78. Last visited June 1, 2008.

Reading group guide to *Blues Dancing. Reading Group Guides.* http://www.reading
groupguides.com/guides_B/blues_dancing1.asp. Last visited June 1, 2008.
Reading group guide to *Leaving Cecil Street. Reading Group Guides.* http://
www.readinggroupguides.com/guides3/leaving_cecil_street1.asp. Last visited June 1, 2008.

Web Sites

"Diane McKinney-Whetstone." *Harper Collins.* http://harpercollins.com/
authors/17683/Diane_McKinneyWhetstone/index.aspx. Publisher's official Web site. Last visited June 1, 2008.
Diane McKinney-Whetstone Official Web Site. http://www.dianemckinney-whetstone.com/. Last visited June 1, 2008.

Terry McMillan (1951–)
African American; Mainstream
Biographical Sketch

Terry McMillan was born on October 18, 1951, in Port Huron, Michigan. She holds a B.S. from the University of California, Berkeley and an M.F.A. from Columbia University. She has won the American Book Award and a National Endowment for the Arts fellowship.

McMillan's character-driven novels feature successful and dynamic African American women searching for fulfillment, be it in their love relationships, their friendships, or their work. *Waiting to Exhale* and *How Stella Got Her Groove Back* were both made into movies. She lives in northern California.

> Everything I write is about empowerment, regardless of what kind it is. It's always about a woman standing up for herself and her rights and her beliefs, and not worrying about what other people think. But one of the things I think fiction should not do is be didactic. I'm not here to preach, I'm not trying to be Gloria Steinem in disguise. I would prefer that you be affected, that by reading something you get a sense of empowerment, and hopefully if it's subtle enough you won't even know it happened. (Terry McMillan, *Writers Yearbook*)

Major Works

Novels

Mama (1987)
Disappearing Acts (1989)
Waiting to Exhale (1992)

How Stella Got Her Groove Back (1996)
A Day Late and a Dollar Short (2001)
The Interruption of Everything (2005)

Research Sources

Encyclopedias and Handbooks: CA; CLC

"Terry McMillan," in *Dictionary of Literary Biography, Volume 292: Twenty-First-Century American Novelists*. Detroit, MI: Gale, 2004. pp. 245–251.

Biographies and Interviews

Bowling, Ann. "Everything I Write is About Empowerment: An Interview with Terry McMillan." *Writers Digest.* March 31, 2001. Available online at http://www.writer-on-line.com/content/view/928/66/~Articles/Fiction-Writing/Everything-I-Write-Is-About-Empowerment:-An-Interview-with-Terry-McMillan.html. Last visited June 1, 2008.

"Exclusive Interview with Best-selling author, Terry McMillan." *Bahamas Weekly.* February 20, 2008. Available online at http://www.youtube.com/watch?v=YVKjaAfjV2Q. Video interview clip.

Gerhart, Ann. "Terry McMillan's Epilogue to 'Groove' Affair." *Washington Post.* June 29, 2005. Available online at http://www.washingtonpost.com/wp-dyn/content/article/2005/06/28/AR2005062801718.html. Last visited June 1, 2008.

Iverem, Esther. "Terry McMillan Q & A." *Seeing Black.* September 26, 2002. http://seeingblack.com/x092602/mcmillan.shtml. Last visited June 1, 2008.

Konkol, Alison, and Mina Ossei. "Terry McMillan." *Voices from the Gaps.* July 22, 1997. http://voices.cla.umn.edu/vg/Bios/entries/mcmillan_terry.html. Last visited June 1, 2008.

Moore, Steve. "A Conversation with Terry McMillan." *Off the Shelf Productions.* 1994. Available online at http://www.womankindflp.org/newletter/interviews/mcmillan.htm. Last visited June 1, 2008.

Criticism and Readers' Guides

Alexander, Amy. "Terry McMillan Takes on 'Ghetto Lit.'" *Nation.* October 15, 2007. Available online at http://www.thenation.com/doc/20071029/alexander. Last visited June 1, 2008.

Reading guide to *A Day Late and a Dollar Short. Penguin.* http://us.penguingroup.com/static/rguides/us/day_late_and_dollar_short.html. Last visited June 1, 2008.

Reading guide to *The Interruption of Everything Penguin.* http://us.penguingroup.com/static/rguides/us/interruption.html Last visited June 1, 2008.

Richards, Paulette. *Terry McMillan: A Critical Companion.* Westport, CT: Greenwood. 1999.

Web Sites

Terry McMillan Official Web Site. http://www.terrymcmillan.com/. Last visited June 1, 2008.
Terry McMillan's Blog. http://www.comment-terry.blogspot.com/. Last visited June 1, 2008.

If You Like Terry McMillan

Terry McMillan's character-driven novels feature successful and dynamic African American women searching for fulfillment, be it in their love relationships, their friendships, or their work.

Then You Might Like

Connie Briscoe. Briscoe's novels are very similar in story to McMillan's, centering on the personal struggles of contemporary, middle-class African American women, covering romantic relationships, work issues, and family.

Pearl Cleage. More on the literary side, Cleage's fiction features strong African American women, social issues, and family/community relationships.

Diane McKinney-Whetstone. McKinney-Whetstone's novels feature strong African American women and generations of close-knit families. They are a bit broader in scope and less romantic than some of MacMillan's, but should still appeal to readers looking for stories about African American women seeking their own identity.

Mameve Medwed
Mainstream
Biographical Sketch

Mameve Medwed was born in Bangor, Maine. She has taught fiction writing classes and workshops, and has told the Springfield City Library, Massachusetts, that "except for one summer taking inventory in an auto parts store, all my work life has revolved around writing—short stories, essays, book reviews, novels, and teaching writing" (http://www.springfieldlibrary.org/massbook_medwed.html). She was a finalist for the Massachusetts Artists Foundation Award in 1985, and her novel *How Elizabeth Barrett Browning Saved My Life* won the 2007 Massachusetts Book Award Honor for Fiction. Her unusual first name, a combination of her grandmother's names, is pronounced "May-Meeve."

Medwed's novels are contemporary and humorous, and feature everyday, younger-middle-aged women dealing with family relationships. Considered modern comedies of manners, they are also very character driven. She lives in Cambridge, Massachusetts.

> I thought I was a short-story writer. Elinor Lipman called and said, you know, you need to write a novel. I told her I didn't know how, and she said, "Nobody does. Take *Mail* and turn it into one." So I did it, kicking and screaming. Then it finds an agent, results in a bidding war, and I thought, this isn't so bad! I felt I never wanted to write short stories again. I love the luxury of working on something for a matter of years. I always panic at the end of a story, worry where the story will go, and will I ever get another idea. Novel writing delays that panic. (Mameve Medwed, http://writersgroupblog.blogspot. com/2008/05/author-spotlight-series-mameve-medwed.html. Last visited June 13, 2008)

Major Works

Novels

Mail (1997)
Host Family (2000)
The End of an Error (2003)
How Elizabeth Barrett Browning Saved My Life (2006)
Men and Their Mothers (2008)

Research Sources

Encyclopedias and Handbooks: CA

Biographies and Interviews

"Making a Case for Comic Fiction." *WGBH.* February 3, 2004. http://forum. wgbh.org/wgbh/forum.php?lecture_id=1470. Last visited June 13, 2008. Audio and video clips of Mewed on a panel interview.
"Mameve Medwed." *Bill Thompson's Eye on Books.* http://www.eyeonbooks. com/ibp.php?ISBN=0446530794. Last visited June 13, 2008. Audio interview clip.
Roveto, Hannah. "Author Spotlight Series: Mameve Medwed." *The Writers Group.* May 7, 2008. http://writersgroupblog.blogspot.com/2008/05/ author-spotlight-series-mameve-medwed.html. Last visited June 13, 2008.
Utah Public Radio. http://stream.publicbroadcasting.net/production/mp3/upr/ local-upr-713075.mp3. Last visited June 13, 2008. Audio interview clip.

Criticism and Readers' Guides

Reading guide for *How Elizabeth Barrett Browning Saved My Life. Harper Collins.* http://www.harpercollins.com/author/authorExtra.aspx?isbn13= 9780060831202&displayType=readingGuide. Last visited June 13, 2008.

Reading guide for *Of Men and Their Mothers. Harper Collins.* http://www.har percollins.com/author/authorExtra.aspx?displayType=readingGuide &isbn13=9780060831219. Last visited June 13, 2008.

Web Sites

"Mameve Medwed." *HarperCollins.* http://www.harpercollins.com/authors/ 29756/Mameve_Medwed/index.aspx. Last visited June 13, 2008. Publisher Web site featuring reading guides.

Mameve Medwed Official Web Site. http://www.mamevemedwed.com/index. php. Last visited June 13, 2008. Features brief bio, several author essays, and book information including reading group guides.

Sue Miller (1943–)
Issue Driven
Biographical Sketch

Sue Miller was born on November 29, 1943, in Chicago. At the age of 16, she was accepted to Radcliffe College. Miller spent several years raising a family as a single mother, working in a day care and teaching creative writing before publishing her first novel to much acclaim in 1986. She is the recipient of a Pushcart Press honorable mention; a National Book Critics Circle Award nomination; a Bunting Institute fellowship; a MacDowell fellowship; and a Guggenheim fellowship.

Miller's novels are "issue-driven," meaning they depict families in crisis, and tackle serious subjects that people think (or hope) will never happen to them. Her emotionally complex characters are often on a search for identity. *The Good Mother* and *Inventing the Abbotts* were made into movies, and *While I Was Gone* was an Oprah's Book Club pick in 2000. Miller lives in Cambridge, Massachusetts.

> I don't know that I'd call what I think I'm doing "conveying a certain message," but certainly the choices are mine, and ones I make because I want the work to have a certain shapeliness, a certain way of making meaning, even if that meaning is something I might not be able to articulate as a message, a moral. As I think of it, the whole book IS the meaning, and I feel responsible for working towards that from the moment I begin to write it. Part of the pleasure in writing for me is to work out how I'm going to have things happen, how I'm going to embody meaning in the events I choose to have take place. (Sue Miller, *The*

Smoking Poet interview, http://thesmokingpoet.tripod.com/id2.html. Last visited June 13, 2008)

Major Works

Novels

The Good Mother (1986)
Family Pictures (1990)
For Love (1993)
The Distinguished Guest (1995)
While I Was Gone (1999)
The World Below (2001)
Lost in the Forest (2005)
The Senator's Wife (2008)

Nonfiction

The Story of My Father: A Memoir (2004)

Short-Story Collection

Inventing the Abbotts and Other Stories (1987)

Research Sources

Encyclopedias and Handbooks: CA

"Sue Miller," in *Dictionary of Literary Biography, Volume 143: American Novelists Since World War II, Third Series*. Detroit, MI: Gale Group, 1994. pp. 151–158.

Biographies and Interviews

"Audio Interview with Sue Miller with Don Swaim, 1990." *Wired for Books.* http://wiredforbooks.org/suemiller/. Last visited June 13, 2008. Audio interview clip.
Fletcher, Ron. "Where Heart Meets Hearth: A Conversation with Sue Miller." *BookPage.* February 1999. Available online at http://www.BookPage.com/9902bp/sue_miller.html. Last visited June 13, 2008.
Hogan, Ron. "Sue Miller." *Beatrice.* http://www.beatrice.com/interviews/miller/. Last visited June 13, 2008.
"An Interview with Sue Miller." *Bookbrowse.* http://www.bookbrowse.com/author_interviews/full/index.cfm?author_number=279. Last visited June 13, 2008.
"Portland Public Library's Brown Bag Lunch Lecture Series—Sue Miller." *Maine Humanities Council.* February 8, 2008. http://mainehumanities.org/

podcasts/index.html. Last visited June 13, 2008. Audio clip of Miller discussing and reading from *The Senator's Wife,* as well as audience Q&A.

Rowland, Russell. "Feature Author: Sue Miller." *The Smoking Poet.* http://thesmokingpoet.tripod.com/id2.html. Last visited June 13, 2008.

"Sue Miller." *Barnes and Noble Meet the Writers.* http://www.barnesandnoble.com/writers/writer.asp?cid=968071. Last visited June 13, 2008. Features audio interview, bibliography, and "If You Like" suggestions.

"Sue Miller." *Bookreporter.* January 25, 2008. http://www.bookreporter.com/authors/au-miller-sue.asp. Last visited June 13, 2008.

Criticism and Readers' Guides

Reading group guide for *The Senator's Wife. Reading Group Guides.* http://www.readinggroupguides.com/guides_S/senators_wife1.asp. Last visited June 1, 2008.

Reading group guide for *While I Was Gone. Reading Group Guides.* http://www.readinggroupguides.com/guides_W/while_i_was_gone1.asp. Last visited June 1, 2008.

"*While I Was Gone* by Sue Miller." *Oprah.com.* http://www.oprah.com/article/oprahsbookclub/pastselections/obc_20000526_aboutauthor/1 Last visited November 26, 2008. Featuring several essays by Miller, discussion questions, and online discussion of *While I Was Gone.*

Web Sites

"Sue Miller Reads from *The Senator's Wife.*" *NPR.* January 22, 2008. http://www.npr.org/templates/story/story.php?storyId=18129589. Last visited June 13, 2008. Links to discussion of *The Senator's Wife* as well as author reading.

Jacquelyn Mitchard (1956–)
Issue Driven
Biographical Sketch

Jacquelyn Mitchard was born on December 10, 1956, in Chicago. As a journalist, she has worked for several papers including the Madison, Wisconsin, *Capital Times,* and the *Milwaukee Journal.* She currently writes a nationally syndicated column, "The Rest of Us." She is the recipient of a Maggie Award for public service magazine journalism, a Milwaukee Press Club Headliner Award, an Anne Powers Award from the Council of Wisconsin Writers, and an Audie Award; she was a Ragdale Foundation Fellow for three years.

While Mitchard was known and respected for her family-oriented column, it was her first novel, *The Deep End of the Ocean,* that made her a success, after it was chosen as the first Oprah Book Club pick in 1996. The novel was also made into a movie starring Michelle Pfeiffer and Whoopi Goldberg in 1999; and was named as 1 of the 10 most influential books of the past 25 years by *USA Today* in 2007. Her novels are characterized by seemingly improbable situations happening to everyday families. She focuses on the connections between women and their families and friends. She also writes novels for young adults that continue in the same issue-driven vein. Mitchard lives outside of Madison, Wisconsin.

I don't think (my books) are sad. They challenging. They're about ordinary people under pressure of extraordinary circumstance. Those pressures reveal people. They reveal character in a way that a great vacation at the beach (unless there is a shark) doesn't. So while I don't think I will always write sad stories. . . I write about what's on my mind and heart—the connections between people, people thrust out of their comfort zones, pity, honor, love, terror. (Jacquelyn Mitchard, http://www.jacquelynmitchard.com/mitchard-qa.htm)

Major Works

Novels

The Deep End of the Ocean (1996)
The Most Wanted (1998)
A Theory of Relativity (2001)
Twelve Times Blessed (2003)
Christmas Present (2003)
The Breakdown Lane (2005)
Cage of Stars (2006)
Still Summer (2007)

Nonfiction

Mother Less Child: The Love Story of a Family (1985)
The Rest of Us: Dispatches from the Mother Ship (1997)

Research Sources

Encyclopedias and Handbooks: CA

Biographies and Interviews

Anderson, Wendy. "An Interview with Jacquelyn Mitchard." *Bookslut.* April 2005. http://www.bookslut.com/features/2005_04_005043.php. Last visited June 13, 2008.

"Jacquelyn Mitchard." *Barnes and Noble Meet the Writers.* http://www.barne sandnoble.com/writers/writer.asp?cid=982645. Last visited June 13, 2008. Features audio interview, bibliography, and "If You Like" suggestions.

"Jacquelyn Mitchard." *Bookreporter.* http://www.bookreporter.com/authors/ au-mitchard-jacquelyn.asp. Last visited June 13, 2008. Brief bio and several interviews.

"Random Q&A: Jacquelyn Mitchard." *The Five Randoms.* May 9, 2008. http://the5randoms.wordpress.com/2008/05/09/random-qa-jacquelyn-mitchard/. Last visited June 13, 2008.

Scribner, Amy. "Jacquelyn Mitchard Captures a Sister's Quest for Revenge." *BookPage.* May 2006. Available online at http://www.BookPage. com/0605bp/jacquelyn_mitchard.html. Last visited June 13, 2008.

Criticism and Readers' Guides

"*The Deep End of the Ocean* by Jacquelyn Mitchard." *Oprah.com.* http://www. oprah.com/article/oprahsbookclub/pastselections/obc_pb_19960917_ about/1. Last visited November 26, 2008. Featuring an essay by Mitchard, discussion questions, and online discussion of *The Deep End of the Ocean.*

Reading group guide for *Christmas, Present. Reading Group Guides.* http:// www.readinggroupguides.com/guides3/christmas_present1.asp. Last visited June 1, 2008.

Reading group guide for *A Theory of Relativity. Reading Group Guides.* http:// www.readinggroupguides.com/guides3/theory_of_relativity1.asp. Last visited June 1, 2008.

Web Sites

Jackie Mitchard's Blog. http://www.jackiemitchard.com/blog/. Last visited June 13, 2008. Author's official blog site.

"Jacquelyn Mitchard." *HarperCollins.* http://www.harpercollins.com/authors/ 20846/Jacquelyn_Mitchard/index.aspx. Last visited June 13, 2008. Publisher's Web site, featuring book information and reading guides.

Jacquelyn Mitchard Official Web Site. http://www.jacquelynmitchard.com/. Last visited June 13, 2008. Features author's blog, essays, discussion boards.

Sarah Mlynowski (1977–)
Chick Lit
Biographical Sketch

Sarah Mlynowski was born on January 4, 1977, in Montreal. After graduating with a degree in English from McGill University, she worked for romance book publishing house Harlequin in the marketing department. Her first novel, *Milkrun,* was the first title in Harlequin's seminal chick lit imprint, Red Dress Ink.

Her novels are classified chick lit, featuring young women trying to make something out of life in the big city. Humorous and realistic, with romantic overtone, they focus on the character's career, friendships, and life outside of her love life as well. Mlynowski also writes a series of magic-themed books for young adults, and has contributed short stories to many chick lit anthologies. She lives in New York City.

> One of the best perks of being published is that I don't have to complete a novel to sell it. I write out an outline and three chapters and hope that someone trusts me enough to buy it. Another perk is that I get to work at home. My commute is eleven seconds. And I can work in my pajamas. Not that I do. But I could. . . . Okay, sometimes I do. I'm pretty sure that wearing pajamas on a regular basis would encourage me to take mid-day naps, which would result in me getting a lot of rest but never finishing a novel. Slippery slope, I tell ya. (Sarah Mlynowski, *Conversations with Famous Writers,* http://conversationsfamouswriters.blogspot. com/2006/08/sarah-mlynowski-see-jane-write-me-vs.html. Last visited June 13, 2008)

Major Works

Novels

Milkrun (2001)
Fishbowl (2002)
As Seen on TV (2003)
Monkey Business (2004)
Me vs. Me (2006)

Nonfiction

Coauthored with Farrin Jacobs. *See Jane Write: A Girl's Guide to Writing Chick Lit* (2006)

Research Sources

Encyclopedias and Handbooks: CA

Biographies and Interviews

Bokma, Cindy. "Sarah Mlynowski." *Conversations with Famous Writers.* August 1, 2006. http://conversationsfamouswriters.blogspot.com/2006/08/sarah-mlynowski-see-jane-write-me-vs.html. Last visited June 13, 2008.

Hogan, Ron. "Lynda Curnyn and Sarah Mlynowski." *Beatrice.* http://www.
    beatrice.com/interviews/reddressink/. Last visited June 13, 2008.
Montgomery, Rian. "Interview with Author Sarah Mlynowski." *Chicklitbooks.*
    http://chicklitbooks.com/author-interviews/interview-with-author-sarah-
    mlynowski/. Last visited June 13, 2008.

Web Sites

"Sarah Mlynowski." *Harlequin.* http://www.eharlequin.com/author.html?
    authorid=824. Last visited June 13, 2007. Publisher's official Web site.
"Sarah Mlynowski." *MySpace.com.* http://profile.myspace.com/index.cfm?fus
    eaction=user.viewprofile&friendid=42009451. Last visited June 13, 2008.
    Author's official MySpace page, featuring blog and updates.
Sarah Mlynowski Official Web Site. http://www.sarahmlynowski.com/. Last
    visited June 13, 2008. Features book information, FAQ.

Mary Alice Monroe
Mainstream
Biographical Sketch

Mary Alice Monroe worked as a journalist and freelance writer before turning to fiction. She earned a B.A. in Asian Studies and Japanese and an M.A.
in Education at Seton Hall University.

Known for her novels set in the South, Monroe focuses her stories on
women dealing with everyday trials and tribulations. She also often puts
an environmental theme in her novels. An active conservationist, she lives
on an island off the coast of South Carolina. She has published romance
novels under the name Mary Alice Kruesi.

> What made me pick up a pen? I can't recall exactly. I've always written
> stories or told them to my eight younger brothers and sisters when it
> was time for bed. I remember enjoying having to write a paper or an
> essay in school. But it wasn't until I was studying Japanese History and
> Culture that I burned to write a novel. In retrospect, I think it was be-
> cause it was the only way I could ever experience life in that period of
> samurai. Old friends remember that I first wanted to write an historical.
> I still haven't finished that novel. But someday I hope I will. (Mary Alice
> Monroe, http://www.likesbooks.com/mam2007.html)

Major Works

Novels

The Long Road Home (1995)
Girl in the Mirror (1998)

The Book Club (2000)
The Four Seasons (2001)
The Beach House (2002)
Skyward (2003)
Sweetgrass (2005)
The Secrets We Keep (2006)
Swimming Lessons (2007)
Time Is a River (2008)

Research Sources

Biographies and Interviews

"Beachbag: Mary Alice Monroe." *Bookreporter.* http://www.bookreporter. com/features/beachbag2005/sweetgrass.asp. Last visited June 26, 2008. Features book review of and excerpt from *Sweetgrass,* and interview.
Brinson, Claudia Smith. "Nature and Nurture." *The South Carolina Slate.* December 11, 2005. Available online at http://www.maryalicemonroe. com/site/epage/33139_67.htm/. Last visited June 26, 2008.
"Mary Alice Monroe Replies." *SeniorNet.* September 1, 2005. http://www.se niornet.org/php/default.php?PageID=7784. Last visited June 26, 2008.
"Quick Q&A with Mary Alice Monroe." *All About Romance.* April 23, 2002. http://www.likesbooks.com/quick30.html. Last visited June 26, 2008.
"Writer's Corner: Mary Alice Monroe." *All About Romance.* May 23, 2007. http://www.likesbooks.com/mam2007.html. Last visited June 26, 2008.

Web Sites

"Mary Alice Monroe." *MySpace.com.* http://profile.myspace.com/index.cfm? fuseaction=user.viewprofile&friendID=19649118. Last visited June 26, 2008. Author's official MySpace page.
Mary Alice Monroe Official Web Site. http://www.maryalicemonroe.com/. Last visited June 26, 2008. Features brief biography and discussion questions for her novels.

Jodi Picoult (1966–)
Issue Driven
Biographical Sketch

Jodi Picoult was born on May 19, 1966, in New York City. She holds a B.A. from Princeton University and a M.A. in Education from Harvard University. Before turning to fiction writing full time, she worked briefly as a junior high teacher. She is the recipient of a New England Book Award for Fiction, a Best Mainstream Fiction Novel designation and a lifetime achievement award from the Romance Writers of America, an Alex Award and an Abraham Lincoln Award for YA fiction in Illinois for *My Sister's Keeper*, and a Fearless Fiction Award from *Cosmopolitan* magazine; and Waterstone Booksellers named her Author of the Year in the United Kingdom in 2007.

Picoult's issue-driven fiction revolves around contemporary women and their families, dealing with a tragedy or some unforeseen, improbable situation. Her books are favorites with discussion groups, as there is always something that seems "ripped from the headlines" in their plots, they confront moral decisions, or they feature "what would you do"–type situations. She has also written several Wonder Woman comic books for DC Comics. *The Pact* and *Plain Truth* have been made into television movies. Picoult lives in Etna, New Hampshire.

> I've always written, my mom says I've written since I was five years old. . . . I always say that the reason that I kept writing is because it's a lot easier than teaching eighth grade English. (Jodi Picoult, http://www.youtube.com/watch?v=Pp5xE8mVm_M. Last visited June 20, 2008)

Major Works

Novels

Songs of the Humpback Whale (1992)
Harvesting the Heart (1994)
Picture Perfect (1995)
Mercy (1995)
The Pact (1998)
Keeping Faith (1999)
Plain Truth (2000)
Salem Falls (2001)
Perfect Match (2002)
Second Glance (2003)
My Sister's Keeper (2004)
Vanishing Acts (2005)
The Tenth Circle (2006)
Nineteen Minutes (2007)
Change of Heart (2008)

Research Sources

Encyclopedias and Handbooks: CA

"Jodi Picoult," in *Dictionary of Literary Biography, Volume 292: Twenty-First-Century American Novelists.* Detroit, MI: Gale, 2004. pp. 278–284.

Biographies and Interviews

Broussard, Rick. "Interview with Jodi Picoult." *New Hampshire Magazine*. Available online at http://www.nh.com/apps/pbcs.dll/article?AID=/20070301/NHM01/70301040/-1/NHM. Last visited June 20, 2008.

Elcik, Catherine. "Hanging with... Jodi Picoult." *The Boston Globe*. April 11, 2008. Available online at http://www.boston.com/ae/books/articles/2008/04/11/jodi_picoult/. Last visited June 20, 2008.

"Jodi Picoult." *Bill Thompson's Eye on Books*. http://www.eyeonbooks.com/ibp.php?ISBN=0743454529. Last visited June 1, 2008. Audio interview clip.

"Jodi Picoult." *Bookreporter*. http://www.bookreporter.com/authors/au-picoult-jodi.asp. Last visited June 20, 2008. Brief bio and several interviews.

MacDonald, Jay. "Graphic Combination." *BookPage*. March 2006. http://www.bookpage.com/0603bp/jodi_picoult.html. Last Visited June 20, 2008.

Matheson, Wendy. "A Chat with... writer Jodi Picoult." *USA Today Pop Candy Blog*. April 11, 2007. http://blogs.usatoday.com/popcandy/2007/04/a_chat_with_wri.html. Last visited June 20, 2008.

Owens, Jill. "Jodi Picoult." *Powells*. March 4, 2008. http://www.powells.com/authors/jodipicoult.html. Last visited June 20, 2008.

Sachs, Andrea. "In Prison with Jodi Picoult." *Time*. February 29, 2008. Available as podcast through link at http://www.time.com/time/magazine/article/0,9171,1718573,00.html. Last visited June 20, 2008.

Criticism and Readers' Guides

Reading group guide for *My Sister's Keeper*. *Reading Group Guides*. http://www.readinggroupguides.com/guides3/my_sisters_keeper1.asp. Last visited June 1, 2008.

Reading group guide for *Nineteen Minutes*. *Reading Group Guides*. http://www.readinggroupguides.com/guides3/nineteen_minutes1.asp. Last visited June 1, 2008.

Web Sites

"At Home with Jodi Picoult." *Turn Here Films*. Available at http://www.youtube.com/watch?v=Pp5xE8mVm_M. Last visited June 20, 2008. Video clip of Picoult discussing her books.

France, Louise. "The Great Unknown." *The Guardian*. April 15, 2007. Available online at http://books.guardian.co.uk/departments/generalfiction/story/0,,2055466,00.html. Last visited June 20, 2008.

Jodi Picoult Official Web Site. http://www.jodipicoult.com/. Last visited June 20, 2008. Features podcasts, photo gallery, links to many interviews, FAQ section.

Jodi Picoult Video Webcast. *Library of Congress.* http://www.loc.gov/book fest/authors/Picoult.html. Last Visited June 20, 2008. Video clip of Picoult at the 2007 National Book Festival.

If You Like Jodi Picoult

Picoult's issue-driven fiction revolves around contemporary women and their families, who are dealing with a tragedy or some unforeseen, improbable situation. Her readers enjoy the thrill of getting to know ordinary people in extraordinary moral circumstances, with plenty of twists and turns. For example, in her novel *My Sister's Keeper,* a young woman, tired of being used for medical donations for her very ill older sister, decides to sue her parents for emancipation.

Then You Might Like

Barbara Delinsky. Delinsky's latest novel *The Secret Between Us* tells the story of a woman who covers for her young daughter in a car accident, with tragic results; and would be a perfect fit for Picoult's fans.

Joy Fielding. Fielding's issue-driven novels center around ordinary women dealing with extraordinary circumstances, and focus on complex issues such as divorce, child abductions, abusive relationships, and fatal illnesses. A good example of this is her novel *Grand Avenue.*

Sue Miller. Miller is more literary than Picoult, but still deals with the same sorts of serious subjects that people never think will happen to them, and with families in crisis.

Jacqueline Mitchard. Mitchard's issue-driven novels, such as *The Deep End of the Ocean* and *A Theory of Relativity* showcase families in turmoil, dealing with difficult or even shocking situations, much like Picoult's work.

Anita Shreve. Shreve's novels feature average characters grappling with extreme situations. A good choice for Picoult's fan would be *The Pilot's Wife,* the story of a woman confronted after her husband's death with his infidelity.

Rosamunde Pilcher (1924–)
Family Stories; Saga
Biographical Sketch

Rosamunde Pilcher was born on September 22, 1924, in Cornwall, England. From 1943 through 1946, she served with the British Women's Royal

Naval Service. In the early1950s she published several light romances under the pen name Jane Fraser. Her novels feature large casts of characters, often families, English and Scottish settings, and gentle, comfortable romance.

Many of her stories have been adapted for television, and are extremely popular in Britain and Germany. *The Shell Seekers* was adapted as a play in 2004. She has also published several nonfiction works about the places in England and Scotland that have inspired her writing. Pilcher's son Robin is also an author, writing family stories much in the same vein as his mother. She currently lives in Scotland.

I always practice my dialogue out loud. . . . Once, when (daughter) Fiona was small, she had a friend over, and I was hanging up the washing and running through my dialogue. Her friend said, "Look, your mummy's lips are moving," and Fiona said, "Don't be stupid. She's writing." (Rosamunde Pilcher, *People* interview, 1990)

Major Works

Novels

A Secret to Tell (1955)
April (1957)
On My Own (1965)
Sleeping Tiger (1967)
Another View (1969)
The End of Summer (1971)
Snow in April (1972)
The Empty House (1973)
The Day of the Storm (1975)
Under Gemini (1976)
Wild Mountain Thyme (1979)
The Carousel (1982)
Voices in Summer (1982)
The Shell Seekers (1988)
September (1990)
Coming Home (1995)
Winter Solstice (2000)

Short-Story Collections

The Blue Bedroom and Other Stories (1985)
Flowers in the Rain and Other Stories (1991)

Research Sources

Encyclopedias and Handbooks: CA; TCRHW

Biographies and Interviews

Butt, Riazat. "Pilcher's Winning Formula." *Manchester Evening News.* February 25, 2004. Available online at http://www.manchestereveningnews. co.uk/entertainment/arts/s/82/82350_pilchers_winning_formula.html. Last visited June 1, 2008.
Hubbard, Kim. "Despite Her Stunning Success in Best-Seller Land, Rosamunde Pilcher's Heart is Still in the Highlands." *People Weekly* May 28, 1990, 89.
"Rosamunde Pilcher." *Bookreporter.* http://www.bookreporter.com/authors/ au-pilcher-rosamunde.asp. August 11, 2000. Last visited January 20, 2008. Author biography and interview.
Smith, Amanda. "Rosamunde Pilcher; In the English Author's Long Career of Writing Romantic Fiction, She Has Never Had a Rejection Slip." *Publishers Weekly* January 29, 1988, 411.

Criticism and Readers' Guides

Contemporary Popular Writers. Detroit, MI: St. James Press, 1997. pp. 322–323.

Web Sites

Rosamunde Pilcher. http://kiswebdesigns.com/rosamundepilcher/news. html. Last visited January 10, 2008. Author's authorized Web site.

Belva Plain (1919–)
Historical; Saga; Women's Romantic Fiction
Biographical Sketch

Belva Plain was born on October 9, 1919, in New York City. She graduated from Barnard College with a degree in history. Before becoming a novelist, Plain wrote short romance stories for many major magazines including *Cosmopolitan, Good Housekeeping, McCall's,* and *Redbook.*

Known for her sweeping, multigenerational sagas, Plain depicts courageous and independent heroines who balance romance with family tragedies and triumphs. Many of her novels are set in different historical time periods such as the Civil War–era and the early 20th century. Her first novel, *Evergreen,* was made into a television miniseries. She currently lives in New Jersey.

> History plays the greatest role in my books—past and current history, because the world is making history every day: in China, in Kosovo, in Pakistan, in Massachusetts, in Nebraska.... Growing up in a world-city

like New York, one is surrounded by people from everywhere. . . . That which most moves me is the courage that led our ancestors to cross that enormous ocean into the unknown. (Belva Plain, http://www.random house.com/features/belvaplain/author.html. Last visited June 20, 2008)

Major Works

Novels

Evergreen (1978)
Random Winds (1980)
Eden Burning (1984)
Crescent City (1984)
The Golden Cup (1986)
Tapestry (1988)
Blessings (1989)
Harvest (1990)
Treasures (1992)
Whispers (1993)
Daybreak (1994)
The Carousel (1995)
Promises (1996)
Secrecy (1997)
Homecoming (1997)
Legacy of Silence (1998)
Fortune's Hand (1999)
After the Fire (2000)
Looking Back (2001)
Her Father's House (2002)
The Sight of the Stars (2003)

Research Sources

Encyclopedias and Handbooks: CA, TCRHW

Biographies and Interviews

"Belva Plain." *Barnes and Noble Meet the Writers.* http://www.barnesand noble. com/writers/writer.asp?cid=881761. Last visited June 13, 2008. Features brief biography, bibliography, and "If You Like" suggestions.

Criticism and Readers' Guides

Contemporary Popular Writers. Detroit, MI: St. James Press, 1997. pp. 324–325
Willens, Susan P. "Plain Storytelling: Belva Plain Discusses Her Fiction." *American Studies International* (36:1) 1998, 40–58.

Web Sites

"Belva Plain." *Random House.* http://www.randomhouse.com/features/belva
plain/. Last visited June 20, 2008. Official publisher Web site, featuring
author Q & A, book information.
"Belva Plain: Born to Write, Born to Love Animals." *Humane Society of
the United States.* http://www.hsus.org/humane_living/memorial_and_
planned_gifts/hsus-special-friends/belva_plain_born_to_write.html.
Last visited June 20, 2008.

Anna Quindlen (1953–)
Issue Driven
Biographical Sketch

Anna Quindlen was born on July 8, 1953, in Philadelphia. She gained national
recognition and a loyal following as a newspaper columnist for the *New York
Times* and as a regular contributor to *Newsweek* magazine. She writes fiction
featuring family issues and women in troublesome situations, such as domestic violence and fatal illnesses. *One True Thing* was made into a movie in 1998,
while *Black and Blue* and *Blessings* were made into television movies. *Black
and Blue* was chosen as an Oprah's Book Club selection in 1998.

Quindlen won the Pulitzer Prize for Commentary in 1992. She lives on the
East Coast.

Major Works

Novels

Object Lessons (1991)
One True Thing (1994)
Black and Blue (1998)
Blessings (2002)
Rise and Shine (2006)

Research Sources

Encyclopedias and Handbooks: CA; CLC

Biographies and Interviews

"Anna Quindlen." *Bookbrowse.* http://www.bookbrowse.com/author_interviews/
full/index.cfm?author_number=293. Last visited September 10, 2008.
"Anna Quindlen." *Bookreporter.* http://www.bookreporter.com/authors/au-
quindlen-anna.asp. Last visited September 20, 2008. Brief biography.
"Anna Quindlen." *Charlie Rose.* October 11, 2006. http://www.charlierose.com/
guests/anna-quindlen. Last visited September 20, 2008. Video interview.

Santora, Alexander M. "Anna Quindlen: From the '60s to the '90s." *Commonweal* (119:3) 1992, 9–13.

Criticism and Reader's Guides

"*Black and Blue* by Anna Quindlen." *Oprah's Book Club.* http://www.oprah. com/article/oprahsbookclub/pastselections/obc_pb_19980409_about/1. Last visited September 26, 2008. Features brief biography, online discussion, and discussion questions.

Web Sites

"Anna Quindlen." *Newsweek.* http://www.newsweek.com/id/32271. Last visited September 11, 2008.
"Anna Quindlen." *Random House.* http://www.randomhouse.com/rhpg/an naquindlen/. Last visited September 20, 2008. Publisher's Web site.
Anna Quindlen Official Web Site. http://www.annaquindlen.com/. Last visited September 11, 1008. Features photos and links to online columns.

Jeanne Ray (1940–)
Light; Women's Romantic Fiction
Biographical Sketch

Jeanne Ray was born in 1940 in Nashville, Tennessee. After 45 years in a nursing career, she turned to a second career as a writer. A registered nurse, she still works one day a week at a clinic in Tennessee. She is the mother of literary novelist Ann Patchett.

Ray's novels take a humorous look at romance among the middle-aged and older generations. The stories portray loving families and realistic situations. Ray lives in Nashville.

> One of the things I was trying to show in *Step-Ball-Change* is that it is possible to have a long, respectable, happy marriage. I wanted to show how complicated even a happy family, a well-adjusted family, if you will, can be, that nothing is ever status quo or comfortable. (Jeanne Ray, *BookPage* interview. http://www.bookpage.com/0205bp/jeanne_ray. html. Last visited June 23, 2008)

Major Works

Novels

Julie and Romeo (2000)
Step-Ball-Change (2002)
Eat Cake (2003)
Julie and Romeo Get Lucky (2005)

Research Sources

Encyclopedias and Handbooks: CA

Biographies and Interviews

Kingsbury, Pam. "A Prescription for Good Reading." *Southern Scribe.* http:// www.southernscribe.com/zine/authors/Ray_Jeanne.htm. Last visited June 23, 2008.

Swilley, Stephanie. "For Jeanne Ray, Writing is All in the Family." *BookPage.* May 2002. http://www.bookpage.com/0205bp/jeanne_ray.html. Last visited June 23, 2008.

Criticism and Readers' Guides

Reading group guide for *Eat Cake. Reading Group Guides.* http://www.read inggroupguides.com/guides3/eat_cake2.asp. Last visited June 23, 2008.

Reading guide for *Julie and Romeo. Penguin.* http://us.penguingroup.com/ static/rguides/us/julie_and_romeo.html. Last visited June 23, 2008.

Web Sites

"Jeanne Ray." *Simon & Schuster.* http://www.simonsays.com/content/destina tion.cfm?tab=3&pid=505606. Last visited June 23, 2008. Publisher Web site.

Luanne Rice (1955–)
Family Stories

Biographical Sketch

Luanne Rice was born on September 25, 1955, in New Britain, Connecticut. She published her first poem at the age of 11, in a local newspaper. When she was 15, *American Girl* magazine published her first short story. Rice is known for her novels showcasing art and ocean themes, and featuring mature, strong female characters. Homecomings, facing responsibilities, and the importance of family are also frequent themes.

Her novels *Crazy in Love, Blue Moon, Follow the Stars Home, Beach Girls,* and *Silver Bells* have been made into television movies. She lives in New York City and Old Lyme, Connecticut.

> As a writer my motto is: don't be afraid of being a fool. And don't worry about what my first grade teacher would think, or the critics, or if the readers will buy this book: all those people. Don't worry about what they're going to think about *anything,* because if I start worrying about those things while I'm writing I'll be so inhibited nothing will come out. (Luanne Rice, *January Magazine* interview. October 2001. http://january magazine.com/profiles/lrice.html. Last visited June 30, 2008)

Major Works

Novels

Angels All Over Town (1985)
Crazy in Love (1988)
Stone Heart (1990)
Secrets of Paris (1991)
Blue Moon (1993)
Home Fires (1995)
Cloud Nine (1999)
Follow the Stars Home (2000)
Dream Country (2001)
Firefly Beach (2001)
Safe Harbor (2002)
True Blue (2002)
Summer Light (2002)
The Perfect Summer (2003)
The Secret Hour (2003)
Silver Bells: A Holiday Tale (2004)
Dance with Me (2004)
Beach Girls (2004)
Summer of Roses (2005)
Summer's Child (2005)
Sandcastles (2006)
The Edge of Winter (2007)
What Matters Most (2007)
Light of the Moon (2008)

Research Sources

Encyclopedias and Handbooks: CA

Biographies and Interviews

"Luanne Rice." *Bookreporter.* http://www.bookreporter.com/authors/au-rice-luanne.asp. Last visited June 30, 2008.

"Luanne Rice." *The Sacramento Bee.* February 7, 2008. http://videos.sacbee.com/vmix_hosted_apps/p/media?id=1712930. Last visited June 21, 2008. Video interview of Rice.

Memmott, Carol. "Five Questions with Luanne Rice." *USA Today.* February 22, 2007. Available online at http://www.usatoday.com/ life/books/news/2007–02–21-luanne-rice_x.htm. Last visited June 30, 2008.

Richards, Linda. "Luanne Rice." *January Magazine.* August 2001. http://januarymagazine.com/profiles/lrice.html. Last visited June 26, 2008.

Criticism and Reader's Guides

Reading group guide for *The Edge of Winter. Reading Group Guides.* http://
www.readinggroupguides.com/guides3/edge_of_winter1.asp Last visited
June 30, 2008.
Reading group guide for *Stone Heart. Reading Group Guides.* http://www.read
inggroupguides.com/guides3/stone_heart1.asp. Last visited June 30, 2008.

Web Sites

Luanne Rice Official Site. http://www.randomhouse.com/features/luannerice/.
Last visited June 30, 2008. Features author blog, book information, and
"Readers Asked" section.
"Luanne Rice on the Power of the Right Poem." *Powells.* http://www.powells.
com/taae/rice.html. Last visited June 30, 2008. Brief essay by Rice.

Nora Roberts (1950–)
Romantic Suspense; Women's Romantic Fiction
Biographical Sketch

Nora Roberts was born on October 10, 1950, in Silver Spring, Maryland.
After working for a few years as a secretary, she tried her hand at romance
writing, and today, with nearly 200 books to her name, she hasn't looked
back since. Roberts has won several Golden Medallions and several Rita
Awards from the Romance Writers of America; was named Best Contemporary Author and has won several Reviewer's Choice Awards from the
Romantic Times; has won the Maggie Award from the Georgia Romance
Writers of America; and was the first author inducted into Romance Writers of America Hall of Fame in 1986. In 1997, it was found that romance
novelist Janet Dailey had plagiarized a number of passages from Robert's
books; in 2008 Roberts accused romance novelist Cassie Edwards of the
same crime.

Roberts writes numerous paperback romance series, some set in historical times and some with mystical or magical elements; under the name J. D.
Robb, she writes a futuristic romantic suspense series. However, the stand-
alone titles she writes as Nora Roberts are best known as contemporary
romantic suspense featuring strong women characters in crisis. She also
writes several paperback series that focus on the trials of different families,
with an emphasis on the women's lives, not just on romance. Many of her
novels have been made into television movies and miniseries. She lives in
Keedysville, Maryland.

The Blizzard of '79, two small children, no morning kindergarten, endless games of Candyland and short supply of chocolate. All of these

things and events led up to me writing my first book. . . I'd always loved to read—and come from a family of readers—but I never thought about writing as a career. I thought everyone made up stories in their heads. During the blizzard, as the radio announced day after day there would be no morning kindergarten, and my horde of Oreos was depleting, I was desperate. To entertain myself I decided to take one of the stories out of my head and write it down. The minute I started, I was hooked. I loved the process of writing. (Nora Roberts, *Writers Write.* http://www.writerswrite.com/journal/jun98/roberts.htm. Last visited June 23, 2008)

Major Works

Novels

Carolina Moon (2000)
The Villa (2001)
Three Fates (2002)
Birthright (2003)
Northern Lights (2004)
Angels Fall (2006)
High Noon (2007)
Tribute (2008)

A full bibliography of Robert's books, including those written as J. D. Robb, can be found on the author's Web site as an annotated Excel spreadsheet, at http://www.noraroberts.com/booklists.htm.

Other Work of Interest

"Nora Roberts Speaks Out On Plagiarism." *Novelists Inc.* http://www.ninc. com/prof_advocacy/nr.asp. Last visited June 23, 2008.

Research Sources

Encyclopedias and Handbooks: CA; TCRHW

Biographies and Interviews

"Author Interview: Nora Roberts." *BookBrowse.* http://www.bookbrowse. com/author_interviews/full/index.cfm?author_number=296. Last visited June 23, 2008.

Elley, Karen Trotter. "Nora Roberts Deals with Destiny in *Three Fates.*" *BookPage.* April 2002. http://www.bookpage.com/0204bp/nora_roberts. html. Last visited June 23, 2008.

"Nora Roberts." *Bookreporter.* http://www.bookreporter.com/authors/au-rob erts-nora.asp. Last visited June 23, 2008. Brief bio and several interviews.

"Nora Roberts Interview: The Thrill of Selling Her First Book." *Lifetime.* Available at http://video.aol.com/video-detail/nora-roberts-interview-the-thrill-of-selling-her-first-book/2820511105. Last visited June 23, 2008.

"Nora Roberts on the Writer's Craft." *Bill Thompson's Eye on Books.* http://www.eyeonbooks.com/icp.php?authID=264. Last visited June 1, 2008. Audio interview clip.

Nuckols, Ben. "For Romance Titan Roberts, Writing Novels is a 9-to-5 Job." August 7, 2006. WTOP News. http://www.wtopnews.com/index.php?nid=25&pid=0&sid=872864&page=1. Last visited June 23, 2008.

"Ten Questions for Nora Roberts." *Time.* November 29, 2007. http://www.time.com/time/magazine/article/0,9171,1689202–1,00.html. Last visited June 23, 2008.

White, Claire. "A Conversation with Nora Roberts." *Writers Write.* June 1998. http://www.writerswrite.com/journal/jun98/roberts.htm. Last visited June 23, 2008.

Criticism and Readers' Guides

Little, Denise, and Laura Hayden, editors. *The Official Nora Roberts Companion.* New York: Berkley, 2002.

Regis, Pamela. "Complicating Romances and Their Readers: Barrier and Point of Ritual Death in Nora Roberts's Category Fiction." *Paradoxa: Studies in World Literary Genres* (3:1–2) 1997, 145–154.

Web Sites

Adwoff. http://adwoff.com/. Last visited June 23, 2008. Roberts-authorized fan site featuring message boards, newsletters, and photographs and travelogues from Robert's vacations.

Nora Roberts Official Web Site. http://www.noraroberts.com. Last visited June 23, 2008. Features full booklist, FAQ, photo gallery.

If You Like Nora Roberts

Nora Robert's contemporary romantic suspense features strong women characters in crisis. Sexual situations are presented explicitly and with candor.

Then You Might Like

Sandra Brown. Brown's novels successfully combine romance elements with mystery, thriller, and romantic suspense. Featuring strong women characters, they are good matches for readers who enjoy Robert's romantic suspense.

Joy Fielding. Several of Fielding's books are romantic suspense, such as *Heartstopper,* the story of a high school teacher set on finding a killer who's targeting teenage girls.

Eileen Goudge. Goudge's romantic suspense novels such *The Woman in Red,* which tells the story of a woman released after nine years in prison for the attempted murder of the drunk driver who killed her son, are generally good choices for Roberts's fans.

Anne B. Ross
Gentle

Biographical Sketch

Ann B. Ross taught literature and the humanities at University of North Carolina, Asheville, before embarking on her writing career.

Although she started writing mysteries, Ross is best known for her "Miss Julia" series, which showcases the eccentric characters and inner workings of a gossipy small town and features the proper yet feisty Southern septuagenarian Miss Julia. Ross lives in Hendersonville, North Carolina.

> [Answering the question, "Are you Miss Julia?"] Absolutely not! I have three children and five grandchildren, she has never had children. She is a widow; I am not. She is wealthy, and I am not. She has learned to speak up for herself, while I am still trying to be sweet and agreeable. One reader wrote, "I am 79 years old, and I want to be like Miss Julia when I grow up." That's my ambition, too. (Ann B. Ross, http://www. missjulia.com/front/faq.html. Last visited June 23, 2008)

Major Works

Novels

The Murder Cure (1978)
The Murder Stroke (1981)
The Pilgrimage (1987)
Miss Julia series: *Miss Julia Speaks Her Mind* (1999), *Miss Julia Takes Over* (2001), *Miss Julia Throws a Wedding* (2002), *Miss Julia Hits the Road* (2003), *Miss Julia Meets Her Match* (2004), *Miss Julia's School of Beauty* (2005), *Miss Julia Stands Her Ground* (2006), *Miss Julia Strikes Back* (2007), *Miss Julia Paints the Town* (2008)

Research Sources

Encyclopedias and Handbooks: CA

Biographies and Interviews

"Ann B. Ross Podcast." *WYPL FM BookTalk.* June 3, 2008. http://wyplf mbooktalk.blogspot.com/2008/06/ann-b-ross-podcast.html. Last visited June 23, 2008.

"Meet the Author: Ann B. Ross" *Public Library of Charlotte and Mecklen-burg County Readers Club.* 2006. http://www.plcmc.org/readers_club/meetAuthor.asp?author=34. Last visited June 23, 2008. Features Q&A and podcast.

Ping, Trisha. "North Carolina Widow Tells All." *BookPage.* April 2008. http://www.bookpage.com/0804bp/ann_b_ross.html. Last visited June 23, 2008.

Criticism and Readers' Guides

Reading group guide for *Miss Julia Speaks Her Mind. Reading Group Guides.* http://www.readinggroupguides.com/guides_M/miss_julia_speaks_her_mind1.asp. Last visited June 23, 2008.

Reading group guide for *Miss Julia Throws a Wedding. Reading Group Guides.* http://www.readinggroupguides.com/guides3/miss_julia_throws_wedding2.asp. Last visited June 23, 2008.

Web Sites

"Ann B. Ross." *HarperCollins.* http://www.harpercollins.com/authors/19268/Ann_B_Ross/index.aspx. Last visited June 23, 2008. Official publisher Web site.

"Ann B. Ross' Profile." *Amazon.com.* http://www.amazon.com/gp/pdp/profile/A1TPFVUUQPT0DO. Last visited June 23, 2008. Features author's blog.

Miss Julia. http://www.missjulia.com/. Last visited June 23, 2008. Official author Web site, featuring book information, FAQ, "book notes," and essays.

Anita Shreve (1946–)
Issue Driven
Biographical Sketch

Anita Shreve was born in 1946 in Massachusetts. She majored in English at Tufts University and worked as a high school teacher and an international journalist. The recipient of an O. Henry Award, a PEN/L. L. Winship Award, and the New England Book Award for fiction, Shreve writes novels that feature strong women characters and explore issues of loss and violence. Decidedly literary in tone, she fits into the issue-driven camp thanks to her tragic themes, yet her focus is on the characters and their feelings, rather than on the dramatic plots.

In 1999, *The Pilot's Wife* was chosen as an Oprah's Book Club selection. *The Weight of Water* was adapted as a movie in 2002; and *The Pilot's Wife* was adapted as a television movie. Shreve lives in Longmeadow, Massachusetts.

I taught for five years . . . I actually liked teaching a lot, but I vividly remember thinking that I had to devote myself full-time to my writing and I had a sense of urgency about it, so I quit midyear to write short stories. (Anita Shreve, http://www.hachettebookgroupusa.com/features/ AnitaShreve/. Last visited June 23, 2008)

Major Works

Novels

Eden Close (1989)
Strange Fits of Passion (1991)
Where or When (1993)
Resistance (1995)
The Weight of Water (1997)
The Pilot's Wife (1998)
Fortune's Rocks (2000)
The Last Time They Met (2001)
Sea Glass (2002)
All He Ever Wanted (2003)
Light on Snow (2004)
A Wedding in December (2005)
Body Surfing (2007)

Research Sources

Encyclopedias and Handbooks: CA

"Anita Shreve," in *Dictionary of Literary Biography, Volume 292: Twenty-First-Century American Novelists.* Detroit, MI: Gale, 2004. pp. 308–313.

Biographies and Interviews

"Anita Shreve." *Authors On The Web.* http://www.Authorsontheweb.com/features/authormonth/0103shreve/shreve.asp. Last visited June 23, 2008. Brief biography and trivia.
"Anita Shreve." *Barnes and Noble Meet the Writers.* http://www.barnesand noble.com/writers/writer.asp?cid=968102. Last visited June 23, 2008. Features interview and book information.
"Anita Shreve." *Bookreporter.* http://www.bookreporter.com/authors/au-shre ve-anita.asp. Last visited June 23, 2008. Features brief biography and interview.
"Author Anita Shreve." *New Hampshire Public Radio.* http://www.nhpr.org/ node/13013. Last visited June 23, 2008. Audio interview clip.

Kanner, Ellen. "Anita Shreve: Telling the Timeless Tale." *BookPage*. December 1999. http://www.bookpage.com/9912bp/anita_shreve.html. Last visited June 23, 2008.

"Listen to Anita Shreve." *Bill Thompson's Eye on Books*. http://www.eyeon books.com/iap.php?authID=613. Last visited June 1, 2008. Audio interview clip.

O'Brien, Catherine. "Anita Shreve: Full Circle with the First Love of My Life." *The Times (London)*. November 3, 2004. Available online at http://www.timesonline.co.uk/tol/life_and_style/article502001.ece. Last visited June 23, 2008.

Criticism and Readers' Guides

"*The Pilot's Wife* by Anita Shreve." *Oprah's Book Club*. http://www.oprah.com/article/oprahsbookclub/pastselections/obc_pb_19990331_about/1. Last visited November 26, 2008. Features brief biography, online discussion, and discussion questions.

Reading group guide for *All He Ever Wanted. Reading Group Guides*. http://www.readinggroupguides.com/guides3/all_he_ever_wanted2.asp. Last visited June 23, 2008.

Reading group guide for *The Pilot's Wife. Reading Group Guides* http://www.read inggroupguides.com/guides_P/pilots_wife1.asp. Last visited June 23, 2008.

Reading group guide for *The Weight of Water. Reading Group Guides*. http://www.readinggroupguides.com/guides3/weight_of_water1.asp. Last visited June 23, 2008.

Web Sites

Anita Shreve Audio Podcast. *Library of Congress*. http://www.loc.gov/today/cyberlc/feature_wdesc.php?rec=3570. Last visited May 22, 2008. Audio clip of Shreve at the 2003 National Book Festival.

Anita Shreve Official Web Site. http://www.hachettebookgroupusa.com/fea tures/AnitaShreve/. Last visited June 23, 2008. Features biography, interview, photo gallery, and "Ask Anita Shreve."

Anita Shreve Video Webcast. *Library of Congress*. http://www.loc.gov/bookfest/2002/shreve.htmlLast visited May 22, 2008. Video clip of Shreve at the 2002 National Book Festival.

Anne Rivers Siddons (1936–)

Mainstream

Biographical Sketch

Anne Rivers Siddons was born on January 9, 1936, in Fairburn, Georgia. After working in advertising and journalism for a number of years, she turned to writing fiction in the mid-1970s. She is the recipient of an Alumna Achievement Award in arts and humanities from Auburn University; was named Georgia Author of the Year in 1988; and received an honorary doctorate from Oglethorpe University. She has also written for magazines, such as *GQ, Georgia, House Beautiful, Redbook,* and *Southern Living.*

Siddons sets her novels in the South. Other than a foray into horror fiction with *The House Next Door,* they generally feature families in crisis and strong women characters. In 1989 her novel *Heartbreak Hotel* was made into the movie *Heart of Dixie. The House Next Door* was made into a television movie in 2006. She currently lives in Charleston, South Carolina.

I think my heroines will always be ordinary women who have made a journey. Maybe it doesn't happen so totally and drastically to most of us, but I haven't seen many women fall into middle age without losing something that has always been a very important part of their lives, and either having to make a life around that, or find a way to go on, or change in order to go on. It seems to me that women are left to do the changing and accommodating. (Anne Rivers Siddons, *BookPage,* http://www.book page.com/9807bp/anne_rivers_siddons.html. Last visited June 23, 2008)

Major Works

Novels

Heartbreak Hotel (1976)
The House Next Door (1978)
Fox's Earth (1981)
Homeplace (1987)
Peachtree Road (1988)
King's Oak (1990)
Outer Banks (1991)
Colony (1992)
Hill Towns (1993)
Downtown (1994)
Fault Lines (1995)
Up Island (1997)
Low Country (1998)
Nora Nora (2000)
Islands (2004)
Sweetwater Creek (2005)
Off Season (2008)

Essay Collection

John Chancellor Makes Me Cry (1975)

Research Sources

Encyclopedias and Handbooks: CA; CLC

Biographies and Interviews

"Anne Rivers Siddons." *Barnes and Noble Meet the Writers.* http://www.bar nesandnoble.com/writers/writer.asp?cid=883628. Last visited June 23, 2008. Features biography and bibliography.

"Anne Rivers Siddons." *New Georgia Encyclopedia.* http://www.georgiaency clopedia.org/nge/Article.jsp?id=h-532. Last visited June 23, 2008.

Cary, Alice. "Anne Rivers Siddons Preserves Natural Treasures in Low Country." *BookPage.* July 1998. http://www.bookpage.com/9807bp/anne_riv ers_siddons.html. Last visited June 23, 2008.

Criticism and Readers' Guides

"Anne Rivers Siddons." *Contemporary Southern Writers.* Detroit, MI: St. James Press, 1999. pp. 330–331.

Reading group guide for *Homeplace. Reading Group Guides.* http://www.reading groupguides.com/guides_H/homeplace1.asp. Last visited June 23, 2008.

Walsh, William. *Speak, So I Shall Know Thee: Interviews with Southern Writers.* Jefferson, NC: McFarland, 1990. p. 242.

York, Lamar. "From Hebe to Hippolyta: Anne Rivers Siddons' Novels." *Southern Literary Journal* (17:2) 1985, 91–99.

Web Sites

"Anne Rivers Siddons." *HarperCollins.* http://www.harpercollins.com/authors/ 9057/Anne_Rivers_Siddons/index.aspx. Last visited June 23, 2008. Official publisher Web site.

Haywood Smith (1949–)
Humorous; Women's Romantic Fiction
Biographical Sketch

Haywood Smith was born in 1949, in Atlanta, Georgia. A former real estate agent, she began writing historical romances in 1996 and turned to comic women's fiction in 2002 with her novel *Queen Bee of Mimosa Branch.* She is the recipient of a Career Achievement Award from *Romantic Times.*

Best known for her Red Hat Club series, Smith writes humorous fiction about sassy, older women. She lives in Buford, Georgia.

I started writing after a midlife assessment in 1989, at my fortieth birthday. Then I found and joined Romance Writers of America's Georgia Chapter in Atlanta, one of the best in the country. There, it took me five years to learn how to "get it right." Then I went to the national RWA conference in New York, and got my agent by signing up for a three-minute pitch session. (Haywood Smith, *Barnes and Noble Meet the Writers.* http://www.barnesandnoble.com/writers/writer.asp?cid=1148231. Last visited June 23, 2008)

Major Works

Novels

Shadows in Velvet (1996)
Secrets in Satin (1997)
Damask Rose (1999)
Dangerous Gifts (1999)
Highland Princess (2000)
Border Lord (2001)
Queen Bee of Mimosa Branch (2002)
Red Hat Trilogy: *The Red Hat Club* (2003), *The Red Hat Club Rides Again* (2005), *Wedding Belles* (2008)

Research Sources

Encyclopedias and Handbooks: CA

Biographies and Interviews

"Haywood Smith." *Barnes and Noble Meet the Writers.* http://www.barnesandnoble.com/writers/writer.asp?cid=1148231. Last visited June 23, 2008. Features biography, interview, and "Good to Know" trivia.
Prince, Dawn G. "N.Y. Times Best Selling Author Haywood Smith on Love, Life and the In-betweens." *Sure Woman.* http://www.surewoman.com/conv/haywood.html. Last visited June 23, 2008.

Criticism and Readers' Guides

Reading group guide for *The Red Hat Club. Reading Group Guides.* http://www.readinggroupguides.com/guides3/red_hat_club2.asp. Last visited June 23, 2008.
Reading group guide for *The Red Hat Club Rides Again. St. Martin's Reading Group Gold.* http://www.readinggroupgold.com/product/product.aspx?isbn=0312990766. Last visited June 23, 2008.

Web Sites

Haywood Smith Official Web Site. http://www.haywoodsmith.net/. Last visited June 23, 2008.

Lee Smith (1944–)

Mainstream

Biographical Sketch

Lee Smith was born on November 1, 1944, in Grundy, Virginia. She has worked as a teacher and a journalist; and is currently a faculty member in the English department of North Carolina State University. Among her accolades and awards are, a Book-of-the-Month Club fellowship; two O. Henry Awards; a Sir Walter Raleigh Award; the North Carolina Award for Literature; a Weatherford Award for Appalachian fiction; a Lyndhurst grant; the Robert Penn Warren Prize for Fiction; a Lila Wallace/*Reader's Digest* Award; an Academy Award in Literature from the American Academy of Arts and Letters; and a Southern Book Critics Circle Award.

Smith's Southern fiction ranges in style, time period, and setting, but each centers on everyday women and their families and friendships, with eccentric characters. She currently lives in Chapel Hill, North Carolina.

Sometimes I stop in the middle of writing a novel and write a story. Short stories seem to have a sense of urgency about them. Like lyric poems, they are more like brief moments of intensity and lend themselves to being written quickly, unlike a novel which has a more leisurely pace. Short stories seem like magic. Young writers often think they must write quickly or lose the magic, but older writers know they won't. They have learned they must rest the mind and imagination. (Lee Smith, *Writers Write.* http://www.writerswrite.com/journal/dec02/lee smith.htm. Last visited June 24, 2008)

Major Works

Novels

The Last Day the Dogbushes Bloomed (1968)
Something in the Wind (1971)
Fancy Strut (1973)
Black Mountain Breakdown (1980)
Oral History (1983)
Family Linen (1985)
Fair and Tender Ladies (1988)
The Devil's Dream (1992)
Saving Grace (1995)
The Christmas Letters: A Novella (1996)
The Last Girls (2002)
On Agate Hill (2006)

Short-Story Collections

Cakewalk (1980)
Me and My Baby View the Eclipse: Stories (1990)
News of the Spirit (1997)

Research Sources

Encyclopedias and Handbooks: CA; CLC

"Lee Smith," in *Dictionary of Literary Biography, Volume 143: American Novelists Since World War II, Third Series*. Detroit, MI: Gale, 1994. pp. 206–216.

Biographies and Interviews

McDaniel, Janet Walker. "Something to Say: An Interview with Lee Smith." *Writers Write*. December 2002. http://www.writerswrite.com/journal/dec02/leesmith.htm. Last visited June 24, 2008.
"Meet the Author: Lee Smith" *Public Library of Charlotte and Mecklenburg County Readers Club*. 2003. http://www.plcmc.org/readers_club/meet Author.asp?author=4. Last visited June 23, 2008. Features Q&A.
Michael Feldman's Whad'ya Know? "Michael Interviews.... Author Lee Smith." May 22, 1999. http://www.notmuch.com/Features/Interview/1999/05.22. html. Last visited June 24, 2008. Audio interview clip.
Southern Literary Review. "Lee Smith." http://www.southernlitreview.com/authors/lee_smith.htm. Last visited June 24, 2008.

Criticism and Readers' Guides

"Lee Smith." *Contemporary Southern Writers*, Detroit, MI: St. James Press, 1999. pp. 336–338.
Reading group guide for *Family Linen*. *Reading Group Guides* http://www.read inggroupguides.com/guides3/family_linen2.asp. Last visited June 24, 2008.
Reading group guide for *On Agate Hill*. *Reading Group Guides* http://www.reading groupguides.com/guides_O/on_agate_hill2.asp. Last visited June 24, 2008.
Smith, Rebecca. *Gender Dynamics in the Fiction of Lee Smith: Examining Language and Narrative Strategies*, San Francisco: International Scholars Publications, 1997.
Tate, Linda. *Conversations with Lee Smith*. Jackson: University Press of Mississippi, 2001.

Web Sites

Lee Smith Official Web Site. http://www.leesmith.com/. Last visited June 24, 2008. Features book information, official biography, several essays.

Danielle Steel
Women's Romantic Fiction
Biographical Sketch

Danielle Steel was born on August 14, 1947, in New York City. In the mid-1970s she worked in advertising and public relations. Now she has written nearly 75 novels, all best sellers. In 2002 Steel was decorated by the French government as an Officier of the distinguished Order of Arts and Letters, for her lifetime contribution to world culture. After dealing with several personal tragedies, including several divorces and the death of a son, Steel became very private, and rarely grants interviews.

While she is often categorized as a romance writer, especially her early paperback releases, most of her novels focus on the lives and relationships of women, not just romance. They tackle dramatic issues such as rape, child abuse, family secrets, and infertility. More than 20 of her novels have been made into television movies and miniseries. Steel has also written two series of children's books. She lives in San Francisco and Paris.

> I'm astonished by my success. I wrote because I needed to and wanted to. It never occurred to me that I'd become famous. I did it at night because I loved it. I never did it to make money, as a job. I just did it because I had to. (Danielle Steel, *The Age (Australia)*. http://www.theage.com.au/articles/2006/03/18/1142582568777.html. Last visited June 24, 2008)

Major Works

Novels

The House on Hope Street (2000)
Journey (2000)
The Kiss (2001)
Leap of Faith (2001)
Lone Eagle (2001)
Answered Prayers (2002)
The Cottage (2002)
Sunset In St. Tropez (2002)
Johnny Angel (2003)
Dating Game (2003)
Safe Harbour (2003)
Ransom (2004)
Echoes (2004)
Miracle (2004)
Second Chance (2004)
Impossible (2005)

Toxic Bachelors (2005)
Bungalow Two (2006)
H.R.H. (2006)
Coming Out (2006)
The House (2006)
Amazing Grace (2007)
Sisters (2007)
Honor Thyself (2008)
Rogue (2008)
A Good Woman (2008)
One Day at a Time (2009)
A full bibliography of Steel's books can be found on the author's Web site, including as a PDF document, at http://www.randomhouse.com/features/steel/bookshelf/steel_chronology.pdf.

Other Works of Interest

His Bright Light: The Story of Nick Traina. New York: Delacorte, 1998. Non-fiction memoir about her son's fatal struggle with bipolar disorder
"A Secret Mission on the Streets." *Newsweek*. June 23, 2008. Available online at http://www.newsweek.com/id/141493. Last visited June 24, 2008.

Research Sources

Encyclopedias and Handbooks: CA; TCRHW

Biographies and Interviews

Angel, Karen. "Lonely Heart." *The Age (Australia)*. March 19, 2006. Available online at http://www.theage.com.au/articles/2006/03/18/1142582568 777.html. Last visited June 24, 2008.
Bane, Vickie L. *The Lives of Danielle Steel: The Unauthorized Biography of America's Number One Best-Selling Author*. New York: St. Martin's Press, 1994.
Bookreporter. "Danielle Steel." http://www.bookreporter.com/authors/austeel-danielle.asp. Last visited June 24, 2008. Brief biography.
"Interview with Danielle Steel." *Amazon.com*. February 28, 2008. http://www.amazon.com/gp/blog/post/PLNKF5GX4XQW3BQG. Last visited June 24, 2008. Audio interview clip.
"Meet the Author: Danielle Steel" *Public Library of Charlotte and Mecklenburg County Readers Club*. 2004. http://www.plcmc.org/readers_club/meetAuthor.asp?author=14. Last visited June 23, 2008. Features Q&A.

Criticism and Readers' Guides

"Danielle Steel," in *Contemporary Popular Writers*. Detroit, MI: St. James Press, 1997. pp. 372–374.

Web Sites

Danielle Steel Official Web Site. http://www.randomhouse.com/features/
  steel/. Last visited June 24, 2008. Features full bibliography, biographical
  information, photo gallery, and "Beyond Books."

If You Like Danielle Steel

Danielle Steel is one of the most well known and most prolific women's fiction authors, with millions of copies sold. Her novels range in place and time,
but always focus on the lives and relationships of women. While she tackles
dramatic issues such as rape, child abuse, family secrets, and infertility, she
also has a romantic tone to her stories.

Then You Might Like

Sandra Brown. Although she currently writes romantic suspense, early Sandra Brown romances, such as *The Rana Look,* which is the story of a su-
permodel's dramatic rise to fame, and *In a Class by Itself,* the story of high
school sweethearts who meet again at their reunion, will likely appeal to
Steel fans.

Barbara Delinsky. Delinsky also blends romance with women's issues. Her
novel *A Woman's Place* features a mother battling a lying ex-husband for custody of her children. Her novel *Family Tree* is the story of a well-off Caucasian
family dealing with family secrets when a child is born with distinctly African
American features.

Eileen Goudge. Goudge's novels feature women dealing with relationships,
often broken friendships or family secrets. They often have to overcome obstacles to their happiness, which is a hallmark of Steel's fiction as well.

Kristen Hannah. Hannah's novels tend to be more tearjerkers than Steel's,
but her stories of family relationships and characters overcoming a variety of
issues will appeal to Steel fans. She writes about love and loss, complicated
relationships, family secrets—themes that Steel shares.

Amy Tan (1952–)
Mainstream
Biographical Sketch

Amy Tan was born on February 19, 1952, in Oakland, California. She received her bachelors and master's degrees in English and linguistics from San
José State University, and after working as a language-development specialist for disabled children, she began writing fiction as a form of therapy. Her
novels feature Chinese American families in conflict and women struggling

with identity issues. Her first novel, *The Joy Luck Club,* was made into a movie in 1993.

She has been the recipient of the Commonwealth Club gold award for fiction; the Bay Area Book Reviewers award for best fiction; and was nominated for a National Book Critics Circle Award, a National Book Award, and a Los Angeles Times Book Award. Tan has chronic Lyme disease and works to raise awareness of the disease.

I wrote an essay called "What the Library Means to Me" when I was eight years old. It was very simple. It said things like "My name is Amy Tan. I'm a third grader at Matanzas School." And then I did what my father always did. He was a minister. I tried to be very sincere, sort of go for the emotion, you know, about how the library is a friend. And this really all was very sincere, but at the end (this is why I think I won this essay contest), I made a pitch for money which, of course, is what ministers do at the end of their talks. And I said how I had given (I think it was) 17 cents, which was my entire life savings at age eight, to the Citizens for Santa Rosa Library, and that I hoped that others would do the same. And so they decided to give me the award. They published my little essay and they gave me a transistor radio and, at that moment, there was a little gleam in mind that maybe writing could be lucrative. (Amy Tan, *Academy of Achievement.* http://www.achievement.org/autodoc/page/tan 0int-1. Last visited March 23, 2009)

Major Works

Novels

The Joy Luck Club (1989)
The Kitchen God's Wife (1991)
The Moon Lady (1992)
The Hundred Secret Senses (1996)
The Bonesetter's Daughter (2001)

Research Sources

Encyclopedias and Handbooks: CA; CLC

Biographies and Interviews

"Amy Tan Biography." *Achievement.* http://www.achievement.org/autodoc/ page/tan0bio-1. Last visited September 20, 2008.
"The Salon Interview: Amy Tan." *Salon.com.* November 1995. http://www. salon.com/12nov1995/feature/tan.html. Last visited September 30, 2008.
Seaman, Donna. "The Booklist Interview: Amy Tan." *Booklist.* (87:3) October 1, 1990, 256–257.

Voices from the Gap. "Amy Tan." December 1996. http://voices.cla.umn.edu/
vg/Bios/entries/tan_amy.html. Last visited September 16, 2008.

Wired for Books. "Audio Interview with Amy Tan with Don Swaim, 1990."
http://wiredforbooks.org/amytan/. Last visited September 19, 2008.
Audio interview clip.

Criticism and Readers' Guides

Braendlin, Bonnie. "Mother/Daughter Dialog(ic)s in, around, and about
Amy Tan's *The Joy Luck Club,*" in *Private Voices, Public Lives: Women
Speak on the Literary Life,* edited by Nancy Owen Nelson. Denton: Uni-
versity of North Texas Press, 1995, pp. 111–124.

Dunick, Lisa M. S. "The silencing effect of canonicity: authorship and the
written word in Amy Tan's novels." *MELUS* (31:2) Summer 2006, 3.

Feng, Pin-Chia. "Amy Tan: Overview," in *Reference Guide to American Literature,* edited by Jim Kamp. 3rd ed. Detroit, MI: St. James Press, 1994.

Huntley, E. D. *Amy Tan: A Critical Companion.* Westport, CT: Greenwood
Press, 1998.

Wenying, Xu. "A Womanist Production of Truths: The Use of Myths in Amy
Tan." *Paintbrush* (22) 1995, 56–66.

Web Sites

Amy Tan's Blog. http://www.redroom.com/author/amy-tan. Last visited September 13, 2008.

Amy Tan Official Web Site. http://www.amytan.net/InterviewWithAmyTan.
aspx. Last visited September 15, 2008. Features Q&A, "Mythology,"
and essays.

Anniina's Amy Tan Page. *Luminarium: Anthology of English Literature.* http://
www.luminarium.org/contemporary/amytan/ Last update October 2007.
Last visited September 30, 2008.

"Featured Author: Amy Tan." *New York Times.* http://www.nytimes.com/
books/01/02/18/specials/tan.html. Last visited September 18, 2008. Features links to book reviews.

Nancy Thayer (1943–)

Humorous

Biographical Sketch

Nancy Thayer was born on December 14, 1943, in Emporia, Kansas. With a
Master's in English from the University of Missouri, she has taught English
in various colleges. Her novels share themes of women's families and friendships, and vary in tone from her more serious first novels to her sassy and
humorous Hot Flash Club series.

An avid library user, Thayer is the cofounder of the Friends of the Nantucket Atheneum. Her novel *Spirit Lost* was made into a movie in 1996. Thayer lives on Nantucket Island, Massachusetts.

Most of my novels involve the theme of families. I'm fascinated by families. (When I was young, I wrote a poem to my sister called "You are the flower, I am the weed.") Even now I can easily spend an hour talking with my blue eyed blond baby sister about whether our father loved her more than me. I probably became a writer from trying to figure out families, but my own children are still an endless sources of mystery, and I don't think I'll ever figure them out. (No doubt a good thing!) (Nancy Thayer, http://www.nancythayer.com/aboutme.html. Last visited June 24, 2008)

Major Works

Novels

Stepping (1980)
Three Women at the Water's Edge (1981)
Bodies and Souls (1983)
Nell (1985)
Morning (1987)
Spirit Lost (1988)
My Dearest Friend (1989)
Everlasting (1991)
Family Secrets (1993)
Belonging (1995)
An Act of Love (1997)
Between Husbands and Friends (1999)
Custody (2001)
"Hot Flash Club" Series: *The Hot Flash Club* (2003), *The Hot Flash Club Strikes Again* (2004), *Hot Flash Holidays* (2005), *The Hot Flash Club Chills Out* (2006)
Moon Shell Beach (2008)

Research Sources

Encyclopedias and Handbooks: CA

Biographies and Interviews

Gray, Joshua. "Nancy Thayer: Always Looking for Inspiration for Another Story Waiting to be Told." *Nantucket Today.* June 2008. Available online at http://www.nantuckettodayonline.com/jun08/nthayer.html. Last visited June 24, 2008.

Lancaster, Mary. "Island Author Nancy Thayer Publishes 18th Novel." *Nantucket Independent.* June 18, 2008. Available online at http://www.nantucketindependent.com/news/2008/0618/the_arts/033.html. Last visited June 24, 2008.

"Local Author Nancy Thayer." *Plum Nantucket.* June 1, 2008. http://nantucket.plumtv.com/videos/local_author_nancy_thayer. Last visited June 24, 2008. Video interview clip.

Criticism and Readers' Guides

Hot Flash Club Discussion Questions. http://www.nancythayer.com/hotflashclubdiscussion.html. Last visited June 24, 2008.

Web Sites

Nancy Thayer Official Web Site. http://www.nancythayer.com/. Last visited June 24, 2008. Features photographs, biography, and newsletter.

Adriana Trigiani
Family Stories
Biographical Sketch

Adriana Trigiani was born in Roseto, Pennsylvania. She worked as a writer on television shows, including *The Cosby Show* and *A Different World,* and has written an off-Broadway play, *Secrets of the Lava Lamp.* Her first novel, *Big Stone Gap,* was inspired by her own life experience. Her Italian immigrant family moved to Big Stone Gap, Virginia, a tiny valley town in the Blue Ridge Mountains, when she was a small child.

Trigiani writes about loving families, usually Italian, and the people in their communities. She has a strong sense of place and of society, and creates vivid characters. She is currently working on a young adult novel. Trigiani lives in New York City.

I've been a full-time writer since 1989. First in television and film, and now in books, with a couple projects per year in film and television still. I started out writing plays for the theater, and I have a feeling that someday I will do something in that arena again. I'm very excited to be working on young adult novels; I'm one of five sisters and my girlfriends are the best. I love writing about the journey, our journey as women. I never know what subject will pique my interest. One of the reasons I love living in New York is that I'm exposed to great stories everyday. (Adriana Trigiani, http://www.adrianatrigiani.com/faq.html. Last visited June 24, 2008)

Major Works

Novels

Big Stone Gap Series: *Big Stone Gap* (2000), *Big Cherry Holler* (2001), *Milk Glass Moon* (2002), *Home to Big Stone Gap* (2006).
Lucia, Lucia (2003)
The Queen of the Big Time (2004)
Rococo (2005)

Research Sources

Encyclopedias and Handbooks: CA

Biographies and Interviews

"Adriana Trigiani." *Barnes and Noble Meet the Writers.* http://www.barnesand noble.com/writers/writer.asp?cid=881791. Last visited June 24, 2008.
"Adriana Trigiani." *Bookreporter.* http://www.bookreporter.com/authors/au-trigiani-adriana.asp. Last visited June 24, 2008. Features brief bio and interviews.
Hammond, Margo, and Ellen Heltzel. "Interview with Adriana Trigiani." *Good Housekeeping.* September 2005. Available online at http://www.goodhousekeeping.com/names/books/books-interview-trigiani-sept05. Last visited June 24, 2008.
Stander, Bella. "A Conversation with Adriana Trigiani." *by Stander.* 2001. http://www.bellastander.com/writer/adriana.htm. Last visited June 24, 2008.

Criticism and Readers' Guides

Reader's guide for *The Queen of the Big Time. Random House.* http://www.randomhouse.com/catalog/display.pperl?isbn=9780812967807&view=rg. Last visited June 24, 2008.
Reading group guide for *Lucia, Lucia. Reading Group Guides.* http://www.read inggroupguides.com/guides3/lucia_lucia1.asp. Last visited June 24, 2008.
Reading group guide for *Rococo. Reading Group Guides.* http://www.reading groupguides.com/guides3/rococo1.asp. Last visited June 24, 2008.

Web Sites

Adriana Trigiani Official Web Site. http://www.adrianatrigiani.com/welcome.html. Last visited June 24, 2008. Features book information, biography, photo album, and "Adriana Answers Your Questions."
Town of Big Stone Gap. http://www.bigstonegap.org/ourtown/trigiani.htm. Last visited June 24, 2008. Official Web site for the real town that inspired Trigiani's series.

Joanna Trollope (1943–)
Family Stories
Biographical Sketch

Joanna Trollope was born on December 9, 1943, in England. Distantly related to 19th-century novelist Anthony Trollope, she received an M.A. from Oxford University and spent time working for the British Foreign Office as well as an English teacher. She is the recipient of a Historical Novel of the Year Award from the Romantic Novelists Association; and an Elizabeth Goudge Historical Award. In 1996, she was appointed the Order of the British Empire for services to literature.

She began her writing career when she published historical romances under the name Caroline Harvey, but she is best known for writing realistic family stories featuring average, middle-class women, set in the modern English countryside. Several of her novels have been adapted for BBC and PBS television broadcasts. Trollope lives in Oxford, England.

> Comparisons with Jane Austen make me twitch. She is a Great: I am a Good—on a good day. . . . I see myself as writing accessible and I hope, thoughtful, contemporary fiction for men and women, about the very dilemmas and situations that they encounter in daily life. (Joanna Trollope, http://www.joan natrollope.com/default.asp?sec=1&sec2=8. Last visited June 25, 2008)

Major Works

Novels

The Choir (1988)
A Village Affair (1989)
A Passionate Man (1990)
The Rector's Wife (1991)
The Men and the Girls (1992)
A Spanish Lover (1993)
Next of Kin (1996)
The Best of Friends (1998)
Other People's Children (1998)
Marrying the Mistress (2000)
Girl from the South (2002)
Brother and Sister (2004)
Second Honeymoon (2006)
Friday Nights (2007)

Other Works of Interest

"Why I Love Chick Lit." *The Guardian (UK)*. http://blogs.guardian.co.uk/
books/2008/06/why_i_love_chicklit.html. June 17, 2008. Last visited June 25,
2008.

Research Sources

Encyclopedias and Handbooks: CA; CLC

"Joanna Trollope," in *Dictionary of Literary Biography, Volume 207: British
Novelists Since 1960, Third Series*. Detroit, MI: Gale, 1999. pp. 294–300.

Biographies and Interviews

Allardice, Lisa. "Profile: Joanna Trollope." *The Guardian (UK)*. February 11,
2006. Available online at http://books.guardian.co.uk/departments/gen
eralfiction/story/0,,1707193,00.html. Last visited June 25, 2008.
"Interview with Joanna Trollope." *Readers Read*. http://www.readersread.
com/features/joannatrollope.htm. Last visited June 25, 2008.
"Joanna Trollope." *Bookreporter*. http://www.bookreporter.com/authors/
au-trollope-joanna.asp. Last visited June 25, 2008. Brief bio and interviews.
"Joanna Trollope." *British Council Arts Group*. http://www.contemporarywri
ters.com/authors/?p=auth02H2L291412634654. Last visited June 25, 2008.
"Joanna Trollope on the Writer's Craft." *Bill Thompson's Eye on Books*. http://
www.eyeonbooks.com/icp.php?authID=521. Last visited June 1, 2008.
Audio interview clip.
Morris, Paula. "She's Middle-Aged, Middle-Brow and Middle-Class, But That's
Enough Compliments." *New Zealand Listener*. April 24, 2004. Available
online at http://www.listener.co.nz/issue/3337/artsbooks/1834/shes_middle-
aged_middle-brow_and_middle-class_but_thats_enough_compliments.ht
ml;jsessionid=6F573C7D8C89EE4D2FA6AB1B8B89A312. Last visited
June 25, 2008.

Criticism and Readers' Guides

Liladhar, Janine. "From the Soap Queen to the Aga-Saga: Different Discur-
sive Frameworks of Familial Femininity in Contemporary 'Women's
Genres.'" *Journal of Gender Studies* (9:1) 2000, 5–12.
Reading group guide for *Friday Nights*. *Reading Group Guides*. http://www.reading
groupguides.com/guides_F/friday_nights1.asp. Last visited June 25, 2008.
Reading group guide for *Marrying the Mistress*. *Reading Group Guides*. http://
www.readinggroupguides.com/guides_M/marrying_the_mistress1.asp.
Last visited June 25, 2008.

Reading guide for *The Girl from the South. Penguin.* http://us.penguingroup. com/static/rguides/us/girl_from_south.html. Last visited June 25, 2008.

Web Sites

Joanna Trollope Official Web Site. http://www.joannatrollope.com/. Last visited June 25, 2008. Features biography, book information, and "Ask Joanna."

If You Like Joanna Trollope

Trollope's family stories featuring average, middle-class women, set in the modern English countryside appeal to readers looking for a good story and believable, familiar characters. Her contemporary domestic stories offer glimpses into everyday life and intelligent, complex characters.

Then You Might Like

Maeve Binchy. Binchy's family stories, particularly early novels such as *The Glass Lake* and *Light a Penny Candle,* will appeal to fans of Trollope's gentle storytelling style as well.

Rosamunde Pilcher. Pilcher's multigenerational sagas, set in the Scottish and English countrysides, have the same warm feel of Trollope's novels. *The Shell Seekers* and *September* would be good read-alike choices.

Luanne Rice. American author Rice's novels may have an entirely different setting than Trollope's, but they do share the same contemporary domestic feel and some of the same themes, such as facing responsibilities and the importance of family, as those of Trollope's.

Marcia Willett. Willett's novels, set in the rural West Country English countryside, feature mature women and their families, and have many of the same characteristics of Trollope's domestic fiction.

Penny Vincenzi (1939–)
Glitz and Glamour
Biographical Sketch

Penny Vincenzi was born on April 10, 1939. She attended secretarial school, and worked at several major magazines, including *Vogue, Cosmopolitan, Tatler,* and *Daily Mirror,* eventually working her way up to fashion editor and journalist.

Vincenzi's glitzy novels cover the jet-setting lives of glamorous women and their high-powered families. She lives in London, England.

I write those sorts of books because they suit my style . . . which is a lot of escapism and lots of lovely accessories for the plot. Some fiction is dose of reality, but mine isn't. (Penny Vincenzi, *Boomerang Books.* http://www.boomerangbooks.com/content/book-news/book-news-archive/interview-with-penny-vinc.shtml. Last visited June 25, 2008)

Major Works

Novels

Old Sins (1989)
Wicked Pleasures (1993)
An Outrageous Affair (1993)
Another Woman (1995)
The Glimpses (1996)
The Dilemma (1996)
Forbidden Places (1996)
Windfall (1997)
Almost a Crime (2006)
Sheer Abandon (2007)
An Absolute Scandal (2007)
The Spoils of Time Trilogy: *No Angel* (2003), *Something Dangerous* (2004), *Into Temptation* (2005)

Research Sources

Encyclopedias and Handbooks: CA

Biographies and Interviews

Fowler, Melissa. "Author of the Month: Penny Vincenzi." *Romance Reader's Connection.* October 2004. http://www.theromancereadersconnection.com/aotm/authorofthemonthvincenzipennyoct04.html. Last visited June 25, 2008.
"Interview with Penny Vincenzi—'It's what I do!'" *Boomerang Books.* July 11, 2005. http://www.boomerangbooks.com/content/book-news/book-news-archive/interview-with-penny-vinc.shtml. Last visited June 25, 2008.
Sale, Jonathan. "My First Job: Novelist Penny Vincenzi was a Harrods Librarian." *The Independent (UK).* April 17, 2008. Available online at http://www.independent.co.uk/student/career-planning/getting-job/my-first-job-novelist-penny-vincenzi-was-a-harrods-librarian-810036.html. Last visited June 25, 2008.

Criticism and Readers' Guides

Discussion questions for *An Absolute Scandal. Reading Group Choices.* http://www.readinggroupchoices.com/search/details.cfm?id=710. Last visited June 25, 2008.

Reader's guide to *Sheer Abandon. Doubleday.* http://doubleday.com/2008/04/28/sheer-abandon-by-penny-vincenzi/. Last visited June 25, 2008.

Web Sites

Penny Vincenzi Official Web Site. http://www.pennyvincenzi.com/. Last visited June 25, 2008. Features brief bio, book information.

"Q & A with Penny Vincenzi." *Goodreads.* http://www.goodreads.com/group/show/4246.Q_A_with_Penny_Vincenzi. Last visited June 25, 2008. Fan message board authorized and moderated by Vincenzi.

Jennifer Weiner (1970–)
Chick Lit

Biographical Sketch

Jennifer Weiner was born on March 28, 1970 in Louisiana. Weiner graduated summa cum laude from Princeton University's creative writing program and worked as a journalist in Pennsylvania and Kentucky before becoming a features writer for the *Philadelphia Inquirer* where she had a successful recurring column dealing with being a twentysomething in the early 1990s.

A staunch defender of chick lit, Weiner is known for giving her characters real personalities and quirks, and for her sense of humor. Her second novel, *In Her Shoes,* was made into a movie in 2005. She lives in Philadelphia.

> I think at this point I could write Beowulf and still have it be called "Chick Lit." That's the risk you run when your first book has naked legs and cheesecake on the cover, a breezy tone and a happy ending (and to be perfectly honest, I probably could not, in fact, write "Beowulf."
>
> . . . From what I've seen and heard, readers could care less what my books are called, how they're reviewed (if they're reviewed at all), where they're shelved or what color the covers are. They just want good stories, funny dialogue, and heroines they can relate to and I hope that's what I deliver. (Jennifer Weiner, *A Moment of Jen.* http://jenniferweiner.blogspot.com/2006_10_22_jenniferweiner_archive.html. Last visited June 25, 2008)

Major Works

Novels

Good In Bed (2001)
In Her Shoes (2002)

Little Earthquakes (2004)
Goodnight Nobody (2005)
Certain Girls (2008)

Short-Story Collection

The Guy Not Taken (2006)

Other Works of Interest

Weiner, Jennifer. "Gray Ladies Up." *Beatrice*. March 9, 2005. http://www.
beatrice.com/archives/001240.html. Last visited June 26, 2008. Essay by
Weiner defending chick lit.

Research Sources

Encyclopedias and Handbooks: CA

Biographies and Interviews

"Author Interview Special: Jennifer Weiner." *Trashionista*. April, 2004.
http://www.trashionista.com/2008/04/author-interv-3.html. Last visited
June 25, 2008.
"Jennifer Weiner." *Barnes and Noble Meet the Writers*. http://www.barne
sandnoble.com/writers/writer.asp?cid=1023373. Last visited June 23,
2008. Features audio interview biography book information.
LaBan, Elizabeth. "An Interview with Jennifer Weiner." *Literary Mama* http://
www.literarymama.com/profiles/archives/000388.html. Last visited June 23,
2008.
Scribner, Amy. "Sleuthing in Suburbia" *BookPage*. October 2005. http://
www.bookpage.com/0510bp/jennifer_weiner.html. Last visited March 10,
2007.

Criticism and Readers' Guides

Reading group guide for *The Guy Not Taken. Reading Group Guides*. http://
www.readinggroupguides.com/guides3/guy_not_taken2.asp. Last visited
June 1, 2008.
Reading group guide for *In Her Shoes. Reading Group Guides*. http://www.
readinggroupguides.com/guides3/in_her_shoes2.asp. Last visited June 1,
2008.

Web Sites

Jennifer Weiner Official Web Site. http://www.jenniferweiner.com/. Last visited June 25, 2008. Includes bibliography, FAQs, and biography.

A Moment of Jen. http://jenniferweiner.blogspot.com/. Last visited June 25, 2008. Weiner's official blog.

MySpace.com. "Jennifer Weiner." http://www.myspace.com/uncanniegirl. Last visited June 25, 2008. Weiner's official MySpace page.

Rebecca Wells (1952–)
Mainstream
Biographical Sketch

Rebecca Wells was born in 1952 in Rapides, Louisiana. She studied writing with the poet Allen Ginsberg, and then began a career as a playwright and actress. She is best known for her trilogy of books featuring the Ya-Ya Sisterhood, a spirited and fun group of women characters who came of age in the American South of the 1940s. She has won the Western States Book Award for fiction and an Adult Trade ABBY Award. Wells suffers from advanced Lyme disease, which she has chronicled on her Web site as keeping her from writing as much as she'd like.

Wells gives readers fully formed, strong female characters, and injects a lot of humor into her stories, while telling dramatic family stories. In 2002, *Divine Secrets of the Ya-Ya Sisterhood* was made into a movie. Wells lives near Seattle, Washington.

> Like most everything in life, writing is sometimes sheer pleasure; sometimes it is pure hell. I come to writing from hearing great stories as a child in Louisiana, where the mark of a person was his or her ability to be a raconteur. I also come as a professional actor. So I see the scenes and hear the voices as I write. Each book is different. (Rebecca Wells, http://ya-ya.com/faq. Last visited June 26, 2008)

Major Works

Novels

Little Altars Everywhere (1992)
Divine Secrets of the Ya-Ya Sisterhood (1996)
Ya-Yas in Bloom (2005)

Research Sources

Encyclopedias and Handbooks: CA

"Rebecca Wells," in *Dictionary of Literary Biography, Volume 292: Twenty-First-Century American Novelists.* Detroit, MI: Gale, 2004. pp. 320–323.

Biographies and Interviews

Bain, Rebecca. "Women Everywhere Embrace the Ya-Ya Sisterhood of Rebecca Wells." *Book Page.* October 1997. http://www.bookpage.com/9710bp/firstperson2.html. Last visited June 26, 2008.

"An Interview with Rebecca Wells." *HarperCollins.* http://www.harpercollins.com/author/authorExtra.aspx?authorID=10439&isbn13=9780060195342&displayType=bookinterview. Last visited June 26, 2008.

"Rebecca Wells." *Barnes and Noble Meet the Authors.* http://www.barnesandnoble.com/writers/writer.asp?cid=968092. Last visited June 26, 2008. Features biography and interview.

"Rebecca Wells." *Bookreporter.* http://www.bookreporter.com/authors/au-wells-rebecca.asp. Last visited June 26, 2008. Brief bio and interviews.

Criticism and Readers' Guides

Reading group guide for *Divine Secrets of the Ya-Ya Sisterhood. Reading Group Guides.* http://www.readinggroupguides.com/guides_D/divine_secrets1.asp. Last visited June 26, 2008.

Reading group guide for *Little Altars Everywhere. Reading Group Guides.* http://www.readinggroupguides.com/guides_L/little_altars_everywhere1.asp. Last visited June 26, 2008.

Reading group guide for *Ya-Yas in Bloom. Reading Group Guides.* http://www.readinggroupguides.com/guides3/yayas_in_bloom1.asp. Last visited June 26, 2008.

Web Sites

Rebecca Wells Official Web Site. http://www.ya-ya.com/. Last visited June 26, 2008. Features book information, message board, and "Ya-Ya Fun."

Marcia Willett
Gentle

Biographical Sketch

Marcia Willett was born on August 6, 1945, in Somerset, England. Before becoming a writer, she studied ballet and worked as a dance instructor. She did not publish her first novel until she was in her fifties.

Her novels, set in the rural West Country English countryside, feature mature women and their families. She lives in Devon, England.

I'm a great inspiration for second careers! When my husband tried to persuade me to write years before, I never particularly wanted to write a book and thought I would have no idea. I always returned to my first love, reading. Eventually he did persuade me . . .When I did start writing, all these ideas and characters were pouring into my mind. In the first couple of years I wrote two books a year. There was so much coming out, I suppose because I started so late there was a lifetime of stuff in there. (Marcia Willett, http://www.marciawillett.co.uk/interview. html. Last visited June 26, 2008)

Major Works

Novels

The Courtyard (1995)
Hattie's Mill (1996)
Second Time Around (1998)
The Chadwick Trilogy: *Looking Forward* (1998), *Holding On* (1999), *Winning Through* (2000)
The Dipper (1999)
Starting Over (1999)
A Week in Winter (2001)
A Summer in the Country (2003)
The Children's Hour (2004)
The Golden Cup (2005)
The Birdcage (2005)
First Friends (2006)
A Friend of the Family (2006)
Echoes of the Dance (2007)
Memories of the Storm (2007)
The Way We Were (2008)

Research Sources

Encyclopedias and Handbooks: CA

Biographies and Interviews

"Interviews: Marcia Willett, The Birdcage." *Transworld.* http://www.booksat transworld.co.uk/catalog/interview.htm?command=search&db=twmain. txt&eqisbndata=0593051238. Last Visited March 23, 2009.

Criticism and Readers' Guides

Reading group guide for *A Friend of the Family. St. Martin's Reading Group Gold.* http://www.readinggroupgold.com/product/product.aspx? isbn=0312306644. Last visited June 26, 2008.

Web Sites

Devonwriters Web Site. http://www.devonwriters.co.uk/. Last visited June 26, 2008. Official Web site of Willett and her husband, Rodney Willett. Includes information about "Marcia Willett's West Country."

Marcia Willett Official Web Site. http://www.marciawillett.co.uk/. Last visited June 26, 2008. Includes interview and "Odds and Ends."

Meg Wolitzer (1959–)
Mainstream
Biographical Sketch

Meg Wolitzer was born on May 28, 1959, in Brooklyn, New York. The recipient of a MacDowell Colony fellowship; a Yaddo residency; a National Endowment for the Arts grant; and a Pushcart Prize, she is known for her literary women's fiction that portray ordinary women's lives and relationships in intimate detail. Her novels also comment on women's roles in society.

Her novel *This Is Your Life* was made into a movie (as *This Is My Life*) in 1992, and *Surrender, Dorothy* was made into a television movie in 2006. Wolitzer also writes children's books. She lives in New York City and teaches at Columbia University.

> I've been publishing for a long time—since I graduated from college in 1981. I've been lucky in that I haven't had too many rejections, but I also haven't exactly been a household name. I think I'm one of those writers who people have heard of, but maybe they aren't sure why. . . . It's important, when you're a writer, to know that there are actually people out there, waiting to read what you write. Without that, you can feel like you're writing only to amuse yourself and your circle of friends, and that can be depressing. (Meg Wolitzer, Barnes and Noble interview, http://www.barnesandnoble.com/writers/writerdetails.asp?cid=975558#interview. Last visited June 26, 2008)

Major Works

Novels

Sleepwalking (1982)
Sparks (1985)
Hidden Pictures (1986)
The Dream Book (1986)
This Is Your Life (1988)
Friends for Life (1994)

Surrender, Dorothy (1999)
The Wife (2003)
The Position (2005)
The Ten-Year Nap (2008)

Other Works of Interest

"In Praise of Pink Ladies." *Beatrice.* March 1, 2005. http://www.beatrice. com/archives/001222.html. Last visited June 26, 2008. Essay by Wolitzer on Chick Lit.

"The Joy of the 1970s." *Powells.* http://www.powells.com/essays/wolitzer.html. Last visited June 26, 2008. Essay by Wolitzer on her novel *The Position.*

Research Sources

Encyclopedias and Handbooks: CA

Biographies and Interviews

"Meg Wolitzer." *Barnes and Noble Meet the Writers.* http://www.barnesand noble.com/writers/writer.asp?cid=975558. Last visited June 26, 2008. Features brief biography and interview.

"Meg Wolitzer on *The Wife*." *Bill Thompson's Eye on Books.* http://www. eyeonbooks.com/ibp.php?ISBN=0684869403. Last visited June 1, 2008. Audio interview clip.

Rich, Mokoto. "Writing About Women Who Are Soccer Moms Without Soccer." *The New York Times.* March 25, 2008. Available online at http://www. nytimes.com/2008/03/25/books/25wolitzer.html?_r=1&oref=slogin. Last visited June 26, 2008.

"*The Ten-Year Nap*: Stay-at-Home Mama Drama." *NPR.* March 24, 2008. http://www.npr.org/templates/story/story.php?storyId=88762428. Last visited June 26, 2008. Audio interview.

Wyrick, Katherine. "Opting Out: Meg Wolitzer on Motherhood and Meaning." *BookPage.* April 2008. http://www.bookpage.com/0804bp/ meg_wolitzer.html. Last visited June 26, 2008.

Criticism and Readers' Guides

Reading guide to *The Ten Year Nap. Penguin.* http://us.penguingroup.com/ static/rguides/us/ten_year_nap.html. Last visited June 26, 2008.

Web Sites

"Meg Wolitzer." *Authors On The Web.* http://www.Authorsontheweb.com/ features/summer03/wolitzer_meg.asp. Last visited June 26, 2008. Features author recommendations.

"Meg Wolitzer's Amazon Blog." *Amazon.com.* http://www.amazon.com/gp/blog/A3JZTPVXXIUPTJ. Last visited June 23, 2008. Features author's blog.

If You Like Meg Wolitzer

Meg Wolitzer's women's fiction is smart and literary, portraying ordinary women's lives and relationships in intimate detail. Her novels also comment on women's roles in society.

Then You Might Like

Elizabeth Berg. Berg's novels focus on relationships, from friends to families to lovers. While not in the same literary style as Wolitzer, her stories about everyday life, tragedies large and small, and the search for happiness in its many forms may appeal to Wolitzer readers.

Alice Hoffman. Another literary writer, Hoffman writes novels that feature strong and intelligent female characters who find their mundane everyday lives disrupted by drama and/or magic. While she differs from Wolitzer in her characterizations and plotlines, Hoffman's use of description and language would likely appeal to readers who appreciate those qualities in Wolitzer's work.

Elinor Lipman. Lipman's novels often deal with family and social issues. Her novels realistically portray their times, and act as social satire, similar to Wolitzer's novels.

Jennifer Weiner. Although Weiner's novels are very different in tone (more on the chick lit–side than serious literary), Weiner's smart writing and keen eye on society puts her on par with Wolitzer, and should appeal to readers who appreciate Wolitzer's social commentary but are looking for something more fun. Weiner's *Little Earthquakes*, an examination of motherhood from the view of four very different women, would be a good choice for Wolitzer fans.

Laura Zigman (1962–)
Chick Lit
Biographical Sketch

Laura Zigman was born on August 11, 1962, in Boston. She received a B.A. from the University of Massachusetts and a certificate in publishing from Harvard University. After working as a publicist for several publishing houses including Random House and Knopf, she became a writer. Her first novel, *Animal Husbandry*, was adapted as the movie *Someone Like You* in 2001.

Zigman's novels are categorized as chick lit, because they feature young women on the cusp of something big—a career, a relationship, or a life choice. However, they are not as light-weight as some of the other titles in the category. Zigman was diagnosed with breast cancer in 2006 and blogs about it at www.healthcentral.com. She lives in Boston.

My publishing background has been useful in understanding how the marketplace works (or doesn't work) when my books have come out. Namely, no matter what you do—what the jacket looks like, what the author photo looks like, how the reviews are—what sells and what doesn't sell in the end is a complete mystery to publishers and booksellers. My background was also useful in understanding what the whole publishing process would be like, from working with an editor to going on tour. But it has not in any way affected what I write about. I write what I write because I'm interested in it. In order to write a whole book about something, you'd better be interested enough in the subject to sustain it for as long as it takes to finish it. (Laura Zigman, *Bookreporter.* http://www.bookre porter.com/authors/au-zigman-laura. asp. Last visited June 26, 2008)

Major Works

Novels

Animal Husbandry (1998)
Dating Big Bird (2000)
Her (2002)
Piece of Work (2006)

Other Works of Interest

"Too Busy to Think About Breast Cancer." *HealthCentral.* http://www.health central.com/breast-cancer/c/8621/29916/breast-cancer. Last visited June 26, 2008. Essay by Zigman on her recovery from breast cancer. Also links to previous Zigman essays on the site.

Research Sources

Encyclopedias and Handbooks: CA

Biographies and Interviews

Adler, Laura Reynolds. "When a New Cow Becomes an Old Cow: Laura Zigman Talks to BookPage about Her New Novel." *BookPage.* January 1998. http://www.bookpage.com/9801bp/firstperson2.html. Last visited June 26, 2008.

Arana, Maria. "Laura Zigman: Just Like Life." *Washington Post*. September 3, 2006. Available online at http://www.washingtonpost.com/wp-dyn/content/article/2006/08/31/AR2006083101159.html. Last visited June 26, 2008.

Hogan, Ron. "The Beatrice Interview: Laura Zigman." *Beatrice.* 1998. http://www.beatrice.com/interviews/zigman/. Last visited June 26, 2008.

"Laura Zigman." *Bookreporter.* http://www.bookreporter.com/authors/au-zigman-laura.asp. Last visited June 26, 2008. Features brief biography and interview.

"Laura Zigman on *Her.*" *Bill Thompson's Eye on Books.* http://www.eyeonbooks.com/ibp.php?ISBN=037541388X. Last visited June 16, 2008. Audio interview clip.

Criticism and Readers' Guides

Reading group guide for *Dating Big Bird. Reading Group Guides.* http://www.readinggroupguides.com/guides_D/dating_big_bird1.asp. Last visited June 26, 2008.

Web Sites

Laura Zigman Official Web Site. http://www.laurazigman.com/. Last visited June 26, 2008. Features biography, bibliography, and blog.

MySpace.com. "Laura Zigman." http://profile.myspace.com/index.cfm?fuseaction=user.viewprofile&friendid=159945500. Last visited June 26, 2008. Zigman's official MySpace page.

List of Authors by Category

The following are some general categories of the types of stories the women's fiction authors in this volume are known for. In addition to getting a quick sense of that sort of books that a given writer publishes, you can also use these lists to find other writers that you might enjoy (i.e., if you enjoy chick lit, you'll see who is known for that type of book). Keep in mind that not all of the authors listed fit into a given category; nor are any of the authors limited to the categories mentioned.

African American

Connie Briscoe
Pearl Cleage
Diane McKinney-Whetstone
Terry McMillan

Chick Lit

Cecelia Ahern
Meg Cabot
Helen Fielding
Jane Green
Marian Keyes
Sophie Kinsella
Sarah Mlynowski

Jennifer Weiner
Laura Zigman

Family Stories

Maeve Binchy
Elizabeth Cadell
Lorna Landvik
Rosamunde Pilcher
Luanne Rice
Adriana Trigiani
Joanna Trollope

Gentle

Maeve Binchy
Jennifer Chiaverini
Fannie Flagg
Lynne Hinton
Ann B. Ross
Marcia Willett

Glitz and Glamour

Jackie Collins
Olivia Goldsmith
Judith Krantz
Penny Vincenzi

Historical

Lois Battle
Barbara Taylor Bradford
Catherine Cookson
Belva Plain

Humorous

Mary Kay Andrews
Meg Cabot
Helen Fielding
Fannie Flagg
Jane Heller

Sophie Kinsella
Lorna Landvik
Haywood Smith
Nancy Thayer

Issue Driven

Barbara Delinsky
Joy Fielding
Sue Miller
Jacquelyn Mitchard
Jodi Picoult
Anna Quindlen
Anita Shreve

Light

Cecelia Ahern
Claire Cook
Katie Fforde
Jeanne Ray

Mainstream

Charlotte Vale Allen
Julia Alvarez
Lois Battle
Elizabeth Berg
Connie Briscoe
Pearl Cleage
Dorothea Benton Frank
Patricia Gaffney
Gail Godwin
Joanne Harris
Alice Hoffman
Ann Hood
Rona Jaffe
Cathy Kelly
Cassandra King
Billie Letts
Elinor Lipman
Jill McCorkle
Terry McMillan

Mameve Medwed
Mary Alice Monroe
Anne Rivers Siddons
Lee Smith
Amy Tan
Rebecca Wells
Meg Wolitzer

Romantic Suspense

Sandra Brown
Joy Fielding
Eileen Goudge
Nora Roberts

Saga

Barbara Taylor Bradford
Elizabeth Cadell
Catherine Cookson
Rosamunde Pilcher
Belva Plain

Women's Romantic Fiction

Mary Kay Andrews
Barbara Taylor Bradford
Sandra Brown
Elizabeth Buchan
Meg Cabot
Claire Cook
Catherine Cookson
Barbara Delinsky
Katie Fforde
Jane Green
Kristin Hannah
Belva Plain
Jeanne Ray
Nora Roberts
Haywood Smith
Danielle Steel

General Bibliography

This listing of general information includes print material, subscription databases, and Web sites of interest.

Encyclopedias and Handbooks

Contemporary Authors. Detroit, MI: Gale, c1962–

Contemporary Literary Criticism. Detroit, MI: Gale, c1973–

Dictionary of Literary Biography. Detroit, MI: Gale, 1981–

Herald, Diana Tixier. *Genreflecting: A Guide to Popular Reading Interests.* Westport, CT: Libraries Unlimited, 2006. Defines genres, including women's fiction, and offers read-alike suggestions.

Lauer, Josh, and Neil Schlager, eds. *Contemporary Novelists.* 7th edition, Detroit, MI: St. James Press, 2000. Includes biographies, bibliographies, and critical essays on approximately 650 contemporary writers.

Mote, Dave, ed. *Contemporary Popular Writers.* Detroit, MI: Gale, 1997. Contains 300 profiles of authors, both living and dead, who were active in the early 1960s or later.

Ramsdell, Kristin. *Romance Fiction: A Guide to the Genre.* Englewood, CO: Libraries Unlimited, 1999. Discusses each of its major categories of romance/women's fiction and tips for reader's advisory and collection development.

Saricks, Joyce G. *The Reader's Advisory Guide to Genre Fiction.* Chicago: American Library Association, 2001. Includes chapter on women's lives and relationships.

Vasudevan, Aruna, ed. *Twentieth-Century Romance and Historical Writers.* 3rd edition, Detroit, MI: St. James Press, 1994. Profiles more than 500 authors who have made significant contributions to romance and historical writing.

Vnuk, Rebecca. *Read On . . . Women's Fiction: Reading Lists for Every Taste.* Westport, CT: Libraries Unlimited, 2009. Annotated booklists of hundreds of contemporary women's fiction titles categorized according to five appeal characteristics.

Databases

Books and Authors. Gale Cengage. http://gale.cengage.com//servlet/ItemDetailServlet?region=9&imprint=000&titleCode=GALE15&cf=n&type=4&id=243609. Last visited June 20, 2008. Reader's advisory database featuring author and book information, read-alike lists, and reviews. Incorporates material from *What Do I Read Next* and other printed reference series published by Gale. Available online as a subscription database only, check your local library for availability.

Literature Resource Center. Gale Cengage. http://www.gale.cengage.com/LitRC. Last visited June 20, 2008. Incorporates material from the *Dictionary of Literary Biography* series, *Contemporary Authors,* and other printed reference series published by Gale. Available online as a subscription database only, check your local library for availability.

Novelist. Ebsco. http://www.ebscohost.com/thisTopic.php?topicID=16&marketID=6. Last visited June 20, 2008. Reader's advisory database featuring author and book information, read-alike lists, articles, essays, and reviews. Available online as a subscription database only, check your local library for availability.

Reader's Advisor Online. Libraries Unlimited/Greenwood. http://rainfo.lu.com/. Last visited June 20, 2008. Reader's advisory database featuring author and book information, read-alike lists, articles, essays, and reviews. Incorporates material from *Genreflecting* series and other printed reference series published by Libraries Unlimited/Greenwood. Available online as a subscription database only, check your local library for availability.

General Web Sites for Readers

Barnes and Noble: Meet the Writers. http://www.barnesandnoble.com/writers/writers2_cds2.asp?PID=1302. Last visited July 1, 2008. Features information on over 500 authors, including author interviews, suggested reading, bibliographies.

Bill Thompson's Eye on Books. http://www.eyeonbooks.com/. Last visited July 1, 2008. Radio broadcaster Thompson has interviewed thousands of authors, and audio clips are available here.

Book Browse. http://www.bookbrowse.com/. Last visited July 1, 2008. Features articles, reviews, and interviews across all genres. Some information is subscription only.

BookPage. http://www.bookpage.com/. Last visited July 1, 2008. Web site of *BookPage,* a monthly book review publication distributed through libraries and bookstores. Features author interviews, book reviews, and articles of interest to readers.

Book Reporter. http://www.bookreporter.com/. Last visited July 1, 2008. Part of the Book Report Network, *Book Reporter* features reviews of newer titles across all genes. Features include articles, author interviews, feature spotlights.

Conversations with Famous Writers. http://conversationsfamouswriters.blogspot. com/. Last visited July 1, 2008. Cindy Bokma interviews contemporary authors in a casual chatty style, including many women's fiction authors. Archived back to 2005.

Fantastic Fiction. http://www.fantasticfiction.co.uk/. Last visited July 1, 2008. Includes bibliographies for over 10,000 authors and nearly 200,000 books. Some entries include author photographs, author recommendations, and images of book jackets. Especially good for chronology and series information.

Fresh Fiction. http://www.freshfiction.com/. Last visited July 1, 2008. Features reviews and interviews across all genres.

GoodReads. http://www.goodreads.com. Last visited July 1, 2008. Social networking site where users can upload and share personal reading lists. Useful to see how readers tag the books they are reading and to get reader-generated reviews. Many authors also now maintain their own pages on GoodReads.

Library of Congress Webcasts. http://www.loc.gov/today/cyberlc/. Last visited July 1, 2008. Video and audio clips of authors presenting at various Library of Congress events.

Library Thing. http://www.librarything.com. Last visited July 1, 2008. Social networking site where users can upload and share personal reading lists. Useful to see how readers tag the books they are reading and to get reader-generated reviews. Many authors also now maintain their own pages on Library Thing.

Mostly Fiction. http://mostlyfiction.com. Last visited July 1, 2008. Reviews of about two dozen newly published books per month, has a section for contemporary fiction , where most of their women's fiction is found. Also searchable by author or title.

Reading Group Guides. http://www.readinggroupguides.com/. Last visited July 1, 2008. Over 2000 reading group guides from across various publishers. Also features useful information on starting and running book discussion groups, and various articles on good reads.

Shelfari. http://www.shelfari.com Last visited July 1, 2008. Social networking site where users can upload and share personal reading lists. Useful to see how readers tag the books they are reading and to get reader-generated reviews. Many authors also now maintain their own pages on Shelfari.

Wired for Books. http://wiredforbooks.org/. Last visited July 1, 2008. *Wired for Books* is a radio program featuring author interviews, and the audio clips are available on this site.

Writers Write. http://www.writerswrite.com/. Last visited July 1, 2008. Features a blog, reviews, and interviews across all genres.

Web Sites Specific to Women's Fiction

All About Romance. http://www.likesbooks.com/. Last visited July 1, 2008. Features reviews, interviews, and message boards; covers women's fiction as well as romance.

Candy Covered Books. http://www.candycoveredbooks.com/. Last visited July 1, 2008. This site gathers reviews of chick lit and women's fiction titles.

Chick Lit Books. http://chicklitbooks.com/. Last visited July 1, 2008. Reviews, author interviews, rankings, and articles about chick lit.

The Road to Romance. http://www.roadtoromance.ca/freestories.htm. Last visited July 1, 2008. Fan-focused site featuring reviews of both major authors and new authors.

Romance Writers of America. http://www.rwanational.org. Last visited July 1, 2008. Features descriptions of category types, reviews, links to author Web sites.

Romantic Times. http://www.romantictimes.com. Last visited July 1, 2008. Online magazine for romance and women's fiction readers, with articles, reviews, and title lists.

Index

About the Author

Photo by Ken Snyder.

REBECCA VNUK has worked as a Readers Advisory Librarian for several libraries and as a Collection Development Specialist for the Chicago Public Library. She is currently the Adult Services Director for the Glen Ellyn Public Library in Illinois. A fiction reviewer for *Library Journal*, she authored their Collection Development feature on chick lit in 2005. She has presented nationally on different readers advisory topics such as chick lit, readers advisory Web sites, and more. She is the 2007–2009 Chairperson of the Adult Reading Round Table, and was named 2008 Fiction Reviewer of the Year for *Library Journal*. She lives in the western suburbs of Chicago.